DATE DUE			

CHAUTAUQUA
SUMMER

CHAUTAUQUA SUMMER

SUMMER

ADVENTURES OF A

LATE-TWENTIETH-CENTURY

VAUDEVILLIAN

Rebecca Chace

Harcourt Brace & Company

New York   San Diego   London

For all of my families
and for Paul

Requests for permission to make copies of any part
of the work should be mailed to: Permissions Department,
Harcourt Brace & Company,
8th Floor, Orlando, Florida 32887.

Library of Congress Cataloging-in-Publication Data
Chace, Rebecca.
Chautauqua summer: adventures of a late-twentieth-century
vaudevillian/by Rebecca Chace.
p.   cm.   .
ISBN 0-15-117011-8
1. Chace, Rebecca.   2. Vaudeville.   3. Entertainers — United
States — Biography.   I. Title.
PN2287.C455A3   1993
792.7′028′092 — dc20   92-33104

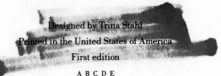

Designed by Trina Stahl
Printed in the United States of America
First edition
A B C D E

"From the first place of liquid darkness, within the second place of air and light, I set down the following record with its mixture of fact and truths and memories of truths and its direction always toward the THIRD PLACE, where the starting place is myth."

JANET FRAME, *An Autobiography*

PREFACE

Someone once said, "All memory is fiction." This book is about my memories of a summer. It is a purely subjective account, but it is true to my own experience, which, in the end, is all one can really know.

ACKNOWLEDGMENTS

I would like first of all to thank my husband, Paul, whose love, encouragement, and support have been constant throughout the writing of this book.

My editor, Anne Freedgood, has been unfailing in her guidance and careful reading of this manuscript. Her suggestions have been crucial to the final shape of the book. My agent, Joseph Spieler, has had faith in my work in its earliest stages, and his enthusiasm has sustained me throughout its composition.

I am forever grateful to others whose criticism, suggestions, and encouragement have helped me in countless ways. These people include above all my father, James Chace; my mother, Jean Valentine; my sister, Sarah Chace; Jennifer Collins; Josh Getzler; and finally my daughter, Pesha Magid, who, in her first year of life, cooperated beautifully with her loving and patient babysitter, Chelsea Jones, to allow me to complete this narrative.

PROLOGUE

EVERYONE IN MY family went to Har-
vard except me. I refused to apply. It was Jula who
told me not to, when I was only eleven. She said it as a
joke, to tease my father, but she said it with a look that
let me know that this would, in fact, be the ultimate
revenge.

Jula was my father's girlfriend. My parents had recently
divorced for the second time. After having been divorced
for a year and a half, they had remarried. In fact, my
parents had four wedding ceremonies. The first one was in
secret, an elopement. Then later there was a big wedding
that everyone was invited to and a bridal dinner at the
Ritz. This first marriage lasted ten years, producing my

older sister, Sarah, and me, and several nervous breakdowns for my mother. I was six years old when they divorced, and about eight years old at the time of their remarriage. This time they had both a religious and a civil ceremony, as my mother had converted to Catholicism. It seemed to run in the family; around the same time I had a set of aunts and uncles who divorced and remarried each other's partners, causing my mother's sister to make her famous remark: "Well, that makes three new marriages and not one new face."

My parents' second marriage lasted less than a year. My mother went back into her patterns of depression, often staying in bed for days at a time. My father had not changed in ways she thought he had, and perhaps, for him, neither had she. Sometime during that year, my father met the woman who was to be the second great love of his life, Julia, or "Jula" as we called her, I'm not sure why.

He moved into a basement apartment on the edge of Spanish Harlem, and Sarah and I spent strangely happy days with him and Jula. Though I was suspicious at first, and ready to bolt if she ever tried to "act like my mother," she was wise enough not to tell us what to do, and in the end I also fell in love with her, as what child could not. She spent hours playing cards and drawing with us. She bought a toy roulette set and taught Sarah and me how to gamble, playing five-card stud, blackjack, and roulette. She was very well off, though she always dressed in jeans, turtlenecks, and sneakers. Most Saturdays she would take us to the Russian Tea Room, where the maitre d' kept a table for her, and I always ordered the same dish: chicken

Kiev. I loved the way the butter and lemon would squirt out as the waiter lanced the tiny breast.

Weekends, we drove to Orchard Beach on City Island to fly kites. Dad, Jula, Sarah, and I, often with my two best friends, Peter and Eli. All of us kids crammed into Dad's blue VW bug. Eli and I, being the smallest, would be crunched into the "back-back" together, and we would all sing the last part of "Hey Jude" together, "Nah, nah, nah, nah, nah, nah nah . . ." while one of the kids, or maybe it was all of us, would scream out the "Hey Jude"s over the chorus. It was Dad and Jula's song. They played the forty-five over and over again that first summer they were together, when I was nine and Sarah was eleven.

Their affair lasted five years. He wanted to marry, but she could never, in the end, bring herself to divorce her husband. I did not understand what barriers there could be between them until much later. She died a year after they broke up, when I was fifteen. Throat cancer. She had always smoked heavily, and much, much later my father explained to me that she had been a severe alcoholic, throwing up quietly in the bathroom in the mornings and starting the day with straight vodka. I never knew, for she wasn't the kind of drunk who became mean or sloppy, but she had always felt too flawed and guilty about her disease to give herself fully to my father, whom she loved so much and who adored her. Perhaps she thought she didn't deserve him, hating herself and unable to break out of the circle she was walking around and around, pushing against the bar of her wheeling addiction.

I had what they called a "checkered" high-school

career. The only thing that really interested me was an after-school improvisational theatre company that I joined for a few years, but our director moved on to bigger and better things, and then there was nothing to relieve the torture of school. I finally ran away from New York with a friend to her parents' summer home on the North Shore of Boston. We enrolled in the local public high school, and I took night classes so that I could graduate a year early. All I could think of was getting out. I had a boyfriend who was already in college, and I visited him every weekend, maintaining only the barest presence at the regional high. But I did graduate in June, to my parents' relief and probably some embarrassment. I was surprised by my acceptance at all of the colleges I applied to. Harvard, of course, where my sister was a freshman, had not been on my list. I suppose the admissions departments at the other universities must have thought of me as an "interesting case." I deferred admission to Barnard College in New York for five years, which is as long as they will let you have the option before they write you off and tell you to make your own way across the street to the adult-education program. Instead of going to college, I hitchhiked across the country with my best friend, Gwen, whom I had met at a boarding school I briefly attended, and we ended up in Seattle.

We were dropped off at the huge public market, which in those days was a mixture of a crafts fair and a farmers' market. There we found a girl who invited us to a party, and this started a chain of circumstances that changed our lives. At the party Gwen met Gene, the man she was to be with for the next four years; he offered to drive us to San Francisco, and by the time we arrived there, they were lovers. Though Gwen and I finished our cross-country trek on the East Coast, we both ended up back in Seattle before the year was out. Gwen enrolled in the University of Washington and set up house with Gene, and I moved into a house peopled by local musicians who were friends of Gene's, who played the clarinet. Through the musicians we met a number of vaudeville performers who came to dance at the gigs and party at the house.

The strange vaudeville world I discovered through them has never let go of me: my West Coast friends are jugglers, sword swallowers, and magicians. From the moment I met them, I wanted to become one of them, and I tried to learn every skill I could get anyone to slow down long enough to teach me. It was at the house that I met my future vaudeville partner, Caitlin. She was a gymnast who had competed for all of her school years until she became disillusioned and dropped out of college, just before I met her. She had a huge head of curls and beautiful wide-set eyes, an exotic face which she grew into more and more as the years passed. I was immediately fascinated by her, and we became inseparable. Deciding on our name was the first step; working up an act would come later. We called ourselves Rosalita and Francesca Devianté: The Daring Devianté Sisters.

There was always a music rehearsal of one sort or another going on downstairs. Rosalita and I were younger than most of the others by a good ten years, and neither of us dared to sing in front of these seasoned musicians who had been fronting rock-and-roll bands for years. So we began to turn to the vaudevillians. Mazuba the Magician was part of our circle, a sallow, melancholy fellow who looked like an N. C. Wyeth illustration and lit up when he performed his sleight of hand. He made a great show of eating a bundle of needles and thread and then, with inexpressible irony, pulling them out of his mouth threaded together into a glittering string. He also worked with live animals—doves and goldfish and rabbits—making them appear and disappear. I never knew how he did it; it is considered impolite to ask a magician how he does something, and he won't tell you in any case. Mazuba was a perfectionist; he would spend weeks working on a prop, adjusting the mechanisms inside a bamboo cane or a false-bottomed top hat.

Through Mazuba we met Samwise, a juggler. His main act at that time was to juggle three clubs while doing a striptease. He was one of those performers you couldn't help liking; his stage presence was totally disarming. Samwise and Mazuba were both employed, with Rosalita and me, for a brief time at the Alligator Palace, a tiny vaudeville theatre in the Skagit Valley north of Seattle, where the land is green and flat.

The Alligator Palace was run by Reverend Chumleigh, who is the closest thing to a hippie version of W. C. Fields I ever encountered, with a brilliant line of patter and a strange collection of vaudeville skills. He was a fire-eater and street performer in the Pacific Northwest for many years, and he is still a local celebrity who also performs all over the country. In those days he was accompanied by his partner, Brodie, Dog of the Future. Brodie was an intelligent little dog who did nothing but sit quietly and play straight man to Chumleigh, most of the time refusing to respond to his commands; it was a great act.

Chumleigh had a dream of revitalizing vaudeville. Back then, land was still very cheap, and he somehow got the money to buy a tiny, narrow building in a small coastal town. He named it the Alligator Palace and staged evenings of vaudeville and occasionally old Marx Brothers movies. He and his wife lived in the back of the theatre, in a room crowded with stacks of books by and about vaudevillians. I devoured his library in the few months I was there.

The Palace lasted for a few years, until Chumleigh was bought out by the neighboring antique store—I can't imagine that he was ever able to break even, but somehow he did scrape by for a while, and his theatre was a tiny mecca for the growing vaudeville movement on the West Coast. Mazuba had asked Rosalita to assist him in an act and brought her with him that summer. She talked Reverend Chumleigh into letting us debut as the Daring Deviante Sisters in the same show. We demonstrated the little acrobatic routine we had worked out, only about five minutes long and not particularly spectacular; but we had a lot of enthusiasm, and I suppose we looked somehow touching in our matching costumes and long curly hair. Chumleigh wasn't exactly full of compliments. He was a sarcastic character who gloomily read aloud from the newspaper every morning, announcing: "The world is going to hell in a handbasket!" But he agreed to give the Devianté Sisters a start in vaudeville: no pay, but room and board. We had our choice of sleeping in a windowless cubby above the stage or a leaking houseboat that was beached on the lawn behind the theatre. We performed two shows a day—when there was an audience.

When there wasn't an audience, we practiced: tumbling, juggling, tap-dancing, anything that we could get people to teach us. Rosalita was already a trained gymnast, and she worked on me. I was never a natural dancer, but I was physically adept and very strong, and Rosalita was a good teacher. I wrote most of the sketches, and we both worked very hard. We learned to juggle clubs in Seattle during a cold, wet February, on an asphalt basketball court near the house, and at first we broke everything in reach. Our hands ached with cold, and the club handles got slipperier and slipperier from being dropped on the wet ground. We hit ourselves in the face with them and in the awful little bones of our wrists, which sent the pain shooting straight up our necks.

One day at the Alligator Palace, Chumleigh volunteered to teach us how to walk a slack rope. A slack rope is like a tightrope, only loose, and made of actual rope or a cloth strap instead of wire. It is much easier for street performing than a tight wire, since all you need are two trees or lampposts to tie onto. On the other hand, walking it is a lot more difficult. The tight wire is like a balance beam; it has some give, but the bounce is quite subtle and fairly easy to control. The slack rope swings both back and forth and up and down, and you have to find a way to go with the swing, or it's all over.

Chumleigh put up the rope between two trees at the

top of a hill in a small park. Learning slack rope inevitably involves a lot of falling, which Chumleigh must have known, but he nevertheless set the rope up where the ground was hard dirt covered with sharp little stones, which seemed to have been raked up by the parks department purposely to discourage people from resting there. Over and over again we fell onto the rocks. I don't know why we didn't ask if we could move to a different spot, where there might have been some grass at least. We were probably too intimidated by Reverend Chumleigh. He, of course, already knew how to walk slack rope, so *he* never fell.

It was during that time that I first met Dmitri, one member of The Flying Karamazov Brothers, a four-man juggling and theatre troupe, which includes Dmitri and Samwise the juggler, now called Smerdyakov Karamazov. The Karamazovs have been an institution for almost twenty years, icons in the counter-culture world that still flourishes on the West Coast; but they have also managed the crossover to the mainstream. They have played Broadway and been in major films, and this gives them an aura in the vaudeville world of marginal incomes and patched-together careers. They support an extended family made up primarily of wives, ex-wives, and girlfriends, all of whom still work for them in various capacities. It seems that a prerequisite of being an employee is having been the lover of one of the Brothers. But this is more a result of the way things fall out than of anything else. The Brothers first came together as an act in the mid-seventies, and everyone had more lovers in those days.

All four are in their mid-thirties or thereabouts and come from the West Coast. Ivan and Dmitri, the original Brothers, were roommates at the University of California at Santa Cruz in the mid-seventies (a classic era for that university) and co-valedictorians for their graduating class. They gave their commencement speech while juggling flaming torches on the podium. All four take their names from Dostoyevsky's book: Dmitri, Ivan, Fyodor, and Smerdyakov. There was originally an Alyosha as well, but he quit several years ago in an attempt to live an ordinary life with his wife and three children.

When we first met at the Alligator Palace, more than a decade ago, The Flying Karamazov Brothers were still starting out, passing the hat at Renaissance Fairs around the country. Dmitri was twenty-four and I was eighteen. He was dark-skinned, with long black hair and eyes that seduced plenty of women. We sat up late in the lee of the beached houseboat and talked. It rained that night, as it did almost every night, and we listened to the water fall around us as we began ten years of almost becoming lovers. Which one of us backed out changed from year to year, but the answer was always no. Dmitri traveled constantly with the troupe, so I didn't get to see him more than a couple of times a year, but he was under my skin somehow; and he stayed there, below the surface, for a long time.

I eventually left Seattle with Rosalita. A friend of ours, Avner the Eccentric, was a silent clown who had studied in Paris, and as soon as he told us about it, we knew we had to go there. My father helped us out, although he would have preferred sending me to college. However, any school was better than nothing, and he was suspicious of the marginal world I was living in out on the Coast. He asked his Parisian contacts about mime and circus schools. One, the Cirque Grusse, a traditional one-ring circus, was on the outskirts of Paris. My father agreed to pay my tuition and give me a small stipend to live on. Rosalita had no money, but we were convinced we could both squeeze by somehow on the money I had, and who knew . . . we might find work over there.

As soon as we arrived, we made our way to the suburban ring that circles Paris, and found the school. It was an old slaughterhouse; huge sculptures of steers adorned the gates. We wandered over to the ring and watched the students work. The women were learning how to balance on big balls in high heels, while the men seemed to be practicing real acrobatics. We immediately decided to change over to the mime half of the school, where we could take classes in circus as part of the curriculum. Neither of us saw ourself tottering around the circus ring in high heels. We wanted to ride the elephants and fly from the trapeze.

After weeks of waking up at dawn and buying *Le Figaro* to look for apartments, we found a two-bedroom flat in Montmartre. Our American boyfriends immediately came over and moved in with us, so there were four people living there, plus Gwen and Gene, who slept in a van in the Bois de Boulogne but cooked, spent their days, washed, and ate with us. The European stint was to bring about the demise of their relationship, however, as it eventually did for most of us. Our Seattle boyfriends were both ten years older than we, rock-and-rollers who were looking for a change after playing the Seattle bar scene. They wanted to come with us, and we wanted them to, for we all were in love. My boyfriend and I sent letters back and forth, counting the days we had to be separated. But as much as I missed my boyfriend before he arrived, I remember being a little taken aback when he actually appeared. Now it was with our men that we took walks by the Seine late at night. It was more of a romantic adventure this way, but we had lost The Daring Devianté Sisters finding their way in this incredible city, leaning over bridges, so full of excitement at just being there that it seemed as if our chests would burst.

Rosalita and I used to sneak out of the Catholic dormitory where we stayed while we were apartment hunting and go roller-skating on the smooth pavements under the Eiffel Tower, screaming through the underground walkways on our skates. Rosalita was always much more my partner in adventure than my boyfriend could possibly be.

We spent our afternoons performing in the big square where all of the street acts worked, at the Centre Georges Pompidou—a strange modern museum with brightly painted pipes as the dominant design motif. Below this weird structure fire-eaters wrapped themselves in chains and shouted drunkenly to the crowd while walking over piles of broken glass. Our boyfriends taught us how to sing, and we did American rock-and-roll with little theatrical sketches built around the songs. I powdered my face heavily with white makeup and wore lipstick the color of dried blood.

After earning the grocery money, which was all the others had to survive on in Paris, Rosalita and I dashed over to the mime school, where we took ballet, mask, and circus classes in a tall, narrow converted carriage house. It was very dark, all the classes were in French, and everybody smoked cigarettes; even while coaching the students on trapeze, our teacher would have a nonfilter stub stuck permanently between his lips. At the entrance to the school sat Lucelle, the concierge, traditionally fat and toad-like in the bottom of the stairwell. She would scream obscenities and gossip at us as we flew past her in our tights, late for class. Lucelle could be charmed, though, and she often overlooked late payments if you simply took the time to stop and talk to her once a week (inquiring, naturally, after her health).

The school was a strange collection of teachers and students. We were the only foreigners except for Belinda, who came from New Zealand and dyed her short blond hair bright green. She was loud and funny, and the three of us became friends. She loathed New Zealand and never wanted to go back. Rosalita and I emulated the French girls, always draped in scarves and cheap jackets, with made-up eyes and lipstick. The ballet class was taught by a woman who seemed on the edge of a nervous collapse. Few of us had had any previous dance training; perhaps that was why. The boys clomped through, and for most of the class she chain-smoked and drank coffee in the corner with the accompanist, complaining in French too rapid for us to understand.

Ismael, a thick, squat black man from North Africa,

13

taught us a combination of martial arts, breathing techniques, and "rhythma": classes where we would sit in a circle and play African drums for an hour and a half. The end was always a relief, for Ismael was relentless. We weren't allowed to talk or ask questions; we were to watch and imitate him. In martial arts he would have us do the same move over and over again for the entire class, until our bodies were so bruised that we went beyond the pain into a sort of meditation. I think that may have been the point, actually. The training made our bodies strong and hard, and by the end of the year our endurance was remarkable. The seeming senselessness of it bothered me, though, as did his silent, powerful intimidation of us. I remember one class where we did nothing but walk on our knees from one end of the room to the other, over and over again, while he stared impassively. Incredibly, one of the tiny Parisians had an affair with Ismael that year—little Sophie, who looked just like Mary Pickford.

Patrice taught mime technique and commedia dell'arte. He was young and classically French-looking, with dark skin, curly hair, and a body that all of the girls talked about. He became a friend, and more than a friend at times, of both Rosalita's and mine. He had us go to the garden behind the Rodin Museum and study the positions of the bronze sculptures. He also told us where we could see *Les Enfants du Paradis*, the greatest French mime film of all time, which stars the master, Jean-Louis Barrault. That theatre, on the far side of town from Montmartre, became my refuge. I would go there alone, over and over again, watching the street performers of turn-of-the-century

Paris depicted by filmmakers who were working under the Vichy government during the occupation.

We spent a year and a half in Paris; then Rosalita and I went on the road with our American troupe, which had by then evolved into a royal family. The Royale Famille DuCaniveaux, we called ourselves—the Royal Family of the Gutter. Our clarinet player, Gene, was the "King," Gwen was the "Queen," Rosalita and I were the "twin Princesses," and our boyfriends, the "Princes"—we were all children of the King and the Queen, so there was plenty of inbreeding in our mythology.

It was the six of us who had originally shared the apartment in Paris, but by the time we landed in a squat house in Amsterdam, tempers were short, and we seemed to be having bad luck with everything. My boyfriend drank more and more; if we started performing at noon, he had to be drunk by that time. He was a brilliant composer and performer, but he didn't believe he could do his act straight. The King slipped a disc and spent all of his time in Amsterdam flat on his back smoking hashish. Things were beginning to unravel between him and Gwen. Rosalita, who had survived a mysterious pelvic disease in Paris, was still painfully thin. When a couple of old friends from Seattle came over to visit us, one of them began to drink again after five years of sobriety and made his girlfriend, and the rest of us, miserable. At the end of the day we collected vegetables off the street where the market was held and made soup.

Street performing in the rain of northern Europe when half of the troupe was sick or drunk was not romantic. I didn't know how to stay with or leave my boyfriend, so when my own body started to show symptoms of the pelvic disease Rosalita had had, I bailed out and flew home. The troupe went in many directions, some to Spain, some to New York, and some, eventually, back to Seattle. Strangely, the troupe never really broke up, but grew to enormous proportions on the West Coast in later years, becoming a legend in our vaudevillian circle. The performances and the name became more of a framework for a family than anything else, and the shows were amateurish but fun. The quality of the performances was always secondary to the group's need to be together.

Back in New York, I auditioned at all of the major theatre schools. I had been on the street, where improvisation is the key to survival as a performer, and I wanted to go back inside the theatre. I was somehow accepted at one of the more prestigious establishments. At my audition I had sung a strange ditty that we used to do on the street, and recited a Shakespearean monologue I remembered from seventh grade. I don't know what they must have thought; probably that I was, again, an "interesting" case.

Thus began three years of unremitting competition, which completely consumed me. Our year started with a class of forty, and fifteen eventually graduated. Despite being one of the survivors, I didn't leave the school with any great sense of confidence: the backstabbing and competition had been too intense for that. Instead, I spent the next few years trying to sort the insecurities and paranoia out of my work and hold onto the training, which had been good.

Training at one of these conservatories has an expected result—commercial work in theatre, film, and television. But somehow, despite my blond curls and good though slightly buck teeth, that world never felt right, and I never quite fit in. So now I find myself hovering at the edge of my third decade, an itinerant trapeze artist performing with a tiny band of vaudevillians and trying to nurse an old Volvo through the scrub lands of Oregon. My life seems to have become as foreign to me as this landscape which shimmers on the horizon as the hot air from the highway meets the day's-end breezes. Dust bouncing off dust turning the windshield to yellow ochre. I've always wanted to be like the heroes of my childhood, D'Artagnan and Huckleberry Finn. I've always believed that one has to strike out somehow and "seek one's fortune," and I've always had the certainty that, like them, I had a secret power: I am the girl who will be rescued by the dwarf when faced with the inevitable but impossible task of spinning flax into gold.

I also suffer from fear of the ordinary, the quotidian; to live an ordinary life has been, above all, my definition of failure. There are certain friends of my childhood who have offices, titles, mortgages on co-ops in Manhattan. When I call them up at work, a secretary answers. Lately, I have begun to envy them. I am no longer the girl who went to the best private school in New York in her navy-blue uniform and studied Latin and French from the age of nine, or the girl who was thrown out of a series of boarding schools in a sort of glory. Things do not always come true as they did in the books, and I have begun to wonder, for the first time, if my life is in fact a charmed one. I find myself watching people on the street, not in New York but in the rest of America, who have regular jobs, which they may not like, but then they never expected to like them. Or maybe they love their jobs; it doesn't really matter, because they have baby strollers and yards and new cars that start up, first time, and I long at times for the ordinary. This frightens me more than anything else, and there is nothing left to do but keep pressing on the gas pedal and hope that I make it safely through another night.

CHAPTER 1

ABOUT A HUNDRED miles from the Idaho border the ground in eastern Oregon breaks up. Ridges of rock not high enough to be called mountains split open the solid, semi-industrialized plate of land. It's always a relief when the land gets too steep and cruel to build on. We're heading east, so the sun is behind us, drawing colors into the cleft horizon. It's a northern evening in midsummer, and the light hangs on to the last ridges as if it will never let go.

Angela has just smoked a joint and is driving a little faster as she slips in an old Beatles tape. The first day I met her, a couple of months ago in New York, she told me about her personal experiences with John Lennon, *after* his death. She made a pilgrimage to the orphanage called "Strawberry Fields" near his childhood home in Liverpool. She snapped some photos, and when they were developed Lennon's face appeared in the shrubbery over the orphanage walls. She showed me the photo—she carries it with her—and I couldn't see Lennon's image. Hating myself for being such a realist, I saw a gray English wall. (I've always wanted to see a ghost, a *real* ghost.) Angela sent a copy of the photo to Yoko, who presumably saw the face, for Angela received a Christmas card that year: a photo of Sean and Yoko and a man dressed in a Santa outfit with a large bag of toys. Sean looks pubescent in the picture, certainly not young enough to be sitting on Santa's lap, and Yoko is wearing enormous dark glasses. Sean and the Santa are laughing while Yoko looks indecipherable. There is a greeting "to Angela" scrawled in one corner, and the whole scene looks very eerie, set against the stark white walls of what one assumes is their spread at the Dakota, the huge, gothic apartment building where John Lennon was shot. I saw the picture, in a pink frame, on the wall of Angela's living room in Seattle and found it somehow frightening.

Angela plays saxophone in the Fighting Instruments of Karma Marching Chamber Band/Orchestra. This band is the heart of the Chautauqua, the vaudeville tour we are both performing in this summer. The band plays Sousa marches and Fellini film scores and is the backbone of the parades that go down Main Street every day we do a show. The Chautauqua exists only for the month-long summer gig, and a couple of benefits during the rest of the year.

Angela has been a member of the band for five years. A sexy, pale-skinned Italian girl from Long Island, she dyes her hair flat black and is the only openly bisexual member of the troupe. She prefers women, though she will often make do with men until the real thing comes along. The last time we saw each other was the first time either of us had gotten really drunk in years. We had stayed up late at my apartment in New York watching *Sid and Nancy* on the VCR and laughing for hours. She threw up, and I remembered why I hardly drink anymore. She is funny and smart, with an East Coast edginess that I feel more comfortable with than the relentless good attitude of some of the Chautauquans. I like Angela because she makes me laugh. Today I'm hoping that we've already talked enough about my not wanting to go to bed with her to drop it for a while. I will turn thirty in six months, and I'm wondering how often what one person wants can possibly coincide with what the other person wants to give. As I glance out the window, I catch a hawk at the instant of folding its wings and dropping straight down at the rock. The line of its body blossoms suddenly into a breakaway glide. I gasp.

"What is it?" asks Angela.

"Nothing. A hawk."

She looks over at me, stoned; we smile. Angela's '73 Volvo, Psycho Car, slows down as we start to climb the pass. I know that the air can't really be getting thinner, but it feels that way. The steering wheel shudders, and the car suddenly pulls to the left. Angela grabs the wheel hard, trying to stay on the road. We make our way to the right lane and pull over just as the car begins to shake and the needle of the temperature gauge shoots way up past the "H." A thin orange line trembling in a zone of infinite, immeasurable heat.

"Shit!" Angela squints hard behind her sunglasses. "Shit."

"What happened?"

"I don't know."

We're shouting at each other over the music. Angela hits the volume knob off and slumps over the wheel. The engine dies, and the dry silence of the scrub lands opens up around us.

"Oh, my God. I can't believe it. Oh, my God."

"What happened, Angela?"

"I can't believe it."

"What is it?"

"I don't know."

I get out and look under the hood. It is easy to know nothing about cars, and so demeaning when that ignorance is total. I check the oil and the battery connections, the two things I know how to do, feeling less and less mechanical as I lean over the engine in my skintight floral-patterned leggings. There is nothing human-scale for miles, and the sun is already starting to leave this stretch of the pass. Once the car cools down, Angela brings out a jug of water to pour into the radiator, which is low, but the engine still won't turn over.

I feel him there before I see him, and when I turn around he is very close. Young-looking, with a pattern of scars across his face and neck that blur his age. He is pressing his hands against his ears as if blocking out some sound, though he appeared in silence. He makes a strange rocking motion as he speaks. I look across the highway and see a white truck pulled over to the side of the road. Never noticed it stopping until he was right there behind us.

"Having trouble? Let me look at your engine. I can help." Words, as if they were threaded together by a normal person, scream out of his mouth. He never stops pressing his hands against his ears, and he starts to walk toward the car.

"No, thanks," I say to him, closing the hood.

I am always polite to people who appear insane. This happens a lot in New York City, but out here it's different, worse. Unlike New York, there's nobody else like him around. Angela stares at me.

"Let's get back in the car. Lock the doors," she whispers.

I ignore her, hoping that he will, too. Growing up in the city has taught me never to acknowledge fear publicly. I keep a distance between us and move slowly. Time is lengthening and changing as if the three of us were in the midst of a car wreck together. He grins as he presses his hands tight over his ears. Angela starts to get in the car.

The cruiser pulls up without blinking its lights, and I find myself smiling uncontrollably at a state trooper. Time speeds up again, and when I turn around the man is gone, across the road, starting up his truck. The trooper is unimpressed by our relief at seeing him and seems completely uninterested in any form of pursuit as the white truck pulls away, but he looks under the hood, checks the same things we did, and agrees to give us a jump start after a brief look at the ashtray inside the car. I don't know what Angela did with the roach, but it's gone. Psycho Car starts up (inexplicably, without a jump start), and he agrees to follow us to the top of the pass.

When I ask Angela to let me drive, she says she's not stoned anymore but moves over to the passenger seat anyway. As we get over the top of the pass, the cruiser disappears into thin air out of the rear-view mirror. There is more light on this side of the ridge, as if we'd gone from evening to afternoon in half a mile. It's easy to lose track of time in this part of the world and to make the wrong assumptions about how much of it has passed. The lack of sleep heightens everything: the diffusion of color and the way the eye rests on the line of the highway. I feel perfectly suspended between car and horizon as I drive, listening to every jolt in the engine while scanning for the green highway sign announcing the rest area.

The Nimbus and the rest area appear simultaneously. The Nimbus is the long yellow school bus owned and operated by Artis the Spoonman. Artis, as they say in New York, is "Whack" (Whacko—it's a compliment). When he plays the spoons, his entire body becomes a rhythm machine. Wooden spoons, silver spoons, tuning forks, flat wooden salad servers—all plucked from his cloth belt of instruments which he lays carefully in front of him on the ground or the stage. Then he simply leaves the earth to play. Objects bounce off of his cheeks, thighs, and hands in a rock-and-roll rhythm. He also writes and sings his poetry, which is confrontational and, at its best, a little frightening. Artis is riveting to watch because he is utterly present onstage, and his energy is raw to the point of transparency.

He's been a part of the Chautauqua since the beginning, eight years ago, and has lived on the road, with no other home, for twenty years. This is a man who has had a domestic life—a wife and children, all gone now—without ever stopping. His bus makes good time on the highway still, so he is the first in the caravan to catch up to us. Angela and I haven't seen anyone else from the troupe for hours. We flash our lights and honk as we turn into the rest area, and The Nimbus lumbers in behind us. Psycho Car and The Nimbus look right together in the clean, well-ordered parking lot: the only two vehicles covered with the light yellow dust that comes from three days at the Oregon Country Fair.

The Fair is the event we have always come home to, where this summer's tour and the first of these Chautauquas began. There is an old vaudeville tradition of celebrating Christmas in July, since performers work the holidays, and we try to make our way back to Oregon every year for the Country Fair. Of course, most vaudevillians then and now seem to be Jewish, so we don't celebrate Christmas, but the family does gather in July.

At the Fair the paths are covered with sweet hay, and craftspeople live on platforms in the trees above their booths. The Long Tom River cups the back boundary of the Fair, and the grass grows high next to its slow-moving brown current. There are always more people sleeping overnight at the Fair than are supposed to be, and always people sleeping with each other who aren't supposed to be. These are the ones who nestle together by the Long Tom, leaving gentle hollows of crushed yellow grass scattered down the banks in the morning.

The Fair lasts for three days but feels longer because nobody sleeps. There are several small stages scattered throughout, as well as the main stage, which has live music going all day. The Flying Karamazov Brothers lead a parade through the entire Fair twice a day. The Karamazovs are the center that holds together the Chautauqua and a small community of vaudevillians who come back to the Country Fair every year. Home base for the Karamazovs and family at the Country Fair is The Circus, a small wooden stage in a glade of trees, and most of the performers who come on the Chautauqua join them there in a loose vaudeville revue.

The Chautauqua tours first began as a way for the performers who put a show together for the Fair to take their community and entertainment on the road. At the Fair there are no critics, no salaries, and nothing to lose. Everyone, in fact, has fun. The parade marches through the Fair, starting from The Circus, twice a day. Fyodor Karamazov takes the lead, spinning clubs over his head and somehow never hitting the feral hippie children who run past on the tiny pathways. Accompanied by the band playing wild parade jazz music, he is followed by stilt walkers, jugglers, rope spinners, and the lady with the famous metal breastplate whose nipples blink on and off as she dances. They march past booths filled with flowers, candles, drums, and bright, rich clothing. Tie-dyed banners and T-shirts are everywhere—echoes of the medieval sixties. All the generations are there. The Fair began in 1969, and on the twentieth anniversary Ken Kesey blew out the candles on an enormous birthday cake that was baked for the occasion. Hulking over the cake, he yelled into the television cameras that the Fair had been taken over by a fascist hippie contingent and the real party was at his farm nearby; everyone was invited.

I had always wanted to go on the Chautauqua, which is an Iroquois word meaning a place where fish are pulled out of the water with a stick. It now also means the month-long journey taken by a band of vaudevillians led by The Flying Karamazov Brothers that leaves from the Country Fair every summer and travels around the Northwest doing vaudeville shows and educational workshops. It's an old name, an old tradition from the turn of the century when there were tent shows out of the town of Chautauqua, New York, which didn't travel at all but presented a week of workshops and evening entertainment that combined variety and education. "Self-betterment" was in fashion then (as it is again now), and the educational aspect was as much of a draw as the entertainment. One could learn about new medical techniques or a romantic phrase in French. The entertainment almost always included a band and an orator. Oratory was a very marketable skill in those days, and famous authors and politicians did the Chautauqua circuit. As they grew in popularity, Chautauquas began not only to spring up in cities all over the country, but also to travel, setting up for a week in every town, like the circus. By the end of the first decade of the twentieth century they had reached their zenith: Teddy Roosevelt declared Chautauquas the most popular form of American entertainment, and they boasted an attendance of thirty million people a year.

That any institution with a name that hard to spell could be so popular still amazes me. If they were big today, someone would surely change the name to "FunFest" or "Millie's Magic Forest." There are older people who come to the show who remember being taken to a Chautauqua as children, as does one of our performers, our folksinger Faith Petric, septuagenarian and self-declared "crone." But the Chautauquas died out with the onset of the moving-picture show, and though there is still an institute in Chautauqua, New York, that presents various events, our Chautauqua is the only one I know of that tours on a regular basis in late-twentieth-century America.

In the fall, I had promised Dmitri Karamazov that I would go on Chautauqua after the Fair. Then in the spring he called me in New York to tell me that the play he was going to write for the show that summer was off, and they would be doing a classic vaudeville revue instead. He had volunteered me as the trapeze artist. I had been studying trapeze in New York, never having given up my vaudeville roots. At my first acting class at the highly competitive conservatory I attended in New York, the teacher asked us what our background in theatre had been. Everyone else had done undergraduate work at various colleges and universities around the country, and they reeled off the titles of school productions of Ibsen, Chekhov, and Shakespeare in which they had appeared. When it came to my turn, I replied simply, "Vaudeville." My teacher stared at me in disbelief.

"Vaudeville is dead," he said.

"No, it's not."

Though he didn't believe me, that season on Broadway saw The Flying Karamazov Brothers, as well as shows by other "new" vaudevillians. *The New York Times* discovered the movement, and everything else, as usual, followed.

I had never done a professional trapeze act, but when Dmitri told me he had volunteered me, I agreed to go. The circus was becoming more and more of an obsession with me, and the trapeze artist is the jewel of the circus ring. The circus community is a small one, and after some asking around I found a French trapeze artist, Jean-Claude, who was willing to help train me for an act that summer. Three times a week I drove out to the suburbs of New York where he lived. He had access to a gym at the university there and had set up a trapeze.

Jean-Claude was a tough teacher. He had had an act with his wife, an American, until she fell, and now he was working as a waiter while stringing together solo trapeze gigs. He obviously wondered how he had ended up in Westchester, a very displaced Parisian. He encouraged me, however, holding my feet as he forced me to do more and more sit-ups every day. I loved to watch him work; he looked like a Maxfield Parrish boy on a swing, leaning farther and farther into it until he dropped suddenly to his ankles. I wasn't ready to do a swinging act yet, so he trained me on the fixed trapeze: it's usually dead-hung about twenty or thirty feet up. My hands quickly became raw with blisters, so I taped them and kept working until the blisters turned to calluses. On the days I stayed in the city, I ran miles in the park and did hundreds of push-ups and sit-ups to condition myself. I was also doing a play that spring and working as an author's research assistant; but trapeze training became my private world. I made only the vaguest of references to what I was doing: until I saw if I could pull it off, I didn't want to talk about it, out of superstition. I loved the discipline and the privacy, and I was proud of my reddened palms, which were badges of a secret society. I sewed a costume all in white, with sequins, and bought rice powder for my face.

The first stop on the Chautauqua was Boise, Idaho, about fourteen hours by car from the Country Fair. It would be roughly twice that for most of the vehicles. I had thought I was doing well to ride in Psycho Car with Angela, that we would keep the pace better than most; and, in fact, even with our breakdown, we were still leading the caravan. No one had passed us, and now Artis told us that he had heard on the CB that The Rubber Chicken (the cook bus) had broken down, and other vehicles were staying to help. No one had been in range of his radio for hours.

We climbed into The Nimbus with Artis for a confer-ence. Jan Luby was making espresso on his stove inside the bus. She was an old friend of Artis and everybody else on the Chautauqua. She was also one half of the singing group "Girls Who Wear Glasses" with Dmitri's ex-wife, Rebo Flordigan. Jan is the only person I have ever met who was actually born in a trunk (her mother was an acrobat, Ruby Luby, and her father was a juggler) and is really from Coney Island.

Two spoons are mounted on either side of The Nimbus's windshield, and the inside whirs and spins with bells, gyroscopes, and toys that play with the light and the wind. The bus has been Artis's home for quite a while, and layers of a life coat the walls and ceiling. At roughly forty, he is a grandfather and has a bumper sticker to prove it, "Happiness is being a Grandparent," wedged in between Country Fair stickers on the back bumper. He doesn't look like a grandfather. His light brown hair ducktails down to his shoulders, and he always wears patchwork clothes, loose, high-waisted Balinese pants and many-pocketed vests. He has a relentless nature and seems to be in perpetual motion. But he still manages to charm, since he is incredibly loving, and he always makes us laugh by constantly berating himself for being both opinionated and egotistical before anyone can beat him to the punch. He is one of those health-food fanatics who is simultaneously addicted to sugar and caffeine, and his moods seem to fly back and forth according to his intake. Jan is wearing a sleeveless flower-print dress which keeps falling off one shoulder as she moves about his kitchen, and she whispers to me later that she isn't wearing any underpants. I don't know whether to believe her or not, but it makes me wonder what the last hundred miles have been like for them. Since the weather is clear, it won't get absolutely dark until ten o'clock, and Artis volunteers to follow us into the closest town, five miles away, to try to find a mechanic who will work after hours.

Baker, Oregon, doesn't look like the kind of place where God touches down too often. One main street, some industrial buildings, one gas station, and one cafe. When we pulled into the gas station a local hippie—possibly the only hippie in town—pulled up on a motorcycle and told us to check out another garage down the street. Hippies in small towns stick together; Artis's bus, Angela's funky old Volvo, and our dusty, colored outfits allowed us into a secret society that presumes a common language—which doesn't always exist. It was clear that he was the town outlaw, and as such we recognized one another. We drove up to an old wooden building with a faded sign, "Broadway Garage." I thought of the Broadway I grew up on: Puerto Rican bodegas and Chinese restaurants. It's all gone now, replaced by boutiques and ice-cream parlors. I snapped a picture of the sign. Artis and Jan went across the street with the hippie to the coffee shop while Angela and I went around to the side of the garage and knocked on the door. An older man was sitting inside in front of a wood stove, which was fired up though it was still warm out, and he watched us silently as we came in and interrupted each other telling what had happened.

"—if he had the time—"

"—we're part of a traveling troupe—"

"—on our way to Boise, to do a show—"

After we ran out of words there was a long pause, and he slowly looked over at the car through the window. Some people like the pace of rural America. I hate it.

"A Volvo?"

He walked over to his bookcase (the only garage I have

ever seen with a sizable bookcase) and found an old Volvo manual. Smiling for the first time, he turned to Angela: "Let's take a look."

He went out to the car with Angela, and they opened up the hood. I went over to the coffee shop. The old hippie was quite soft-spoken, with a baseball hat that said, "Old Bikers Never Die, They Just Get Harder." I kept glancing back at the phrase, inadvertently. After the second cup I went over to check on Angela. I saw her and the mechanic sitting together in the front seat of Psycho Car. The engine was turned off, and Angela was smiling. I stopped, not quite sure why; there was something in the way she was holding herself that I had never seen before. She turned and saw me, rolled down the window, and called me over.

"It was just the distributor cap."

"Oh, great . . . *is* that great?"

"Yeah! Everything's gonna be fine. We fixed it."

They got out of the car, and she thanked him as they walked back to the office. I suddenly saw the polite Catholic girl she must have been. A gray skirt with a white blouse and dark green knee socks, two long braids, hair parted down the middle. Now her black lace bra showed through her torn white T-shirt with studied sexiness.

"How much was it?" I asked when he had gone.

"Nothing."

"He didn't charge anything?"

"No."

Angela was not a calm person. All of a sudden she seemed too quiet and gentle.

"What happened?"

"He fixed the distributor cap, and we talked about God."

"God?"

"Yeah. He said he had read the Bible in five different versions and finally decided on the Mormon Bible. But not because he was a Mormon, just because he liked that version the best."

I stared at her. "You mean, he preached to you while he fixed the car?"

"No, no, he didn't preach. We just talked about God. Not even any particular religion. Just what it meant to have faith. It really was, I don't know . . . simple."

Her voice was on the edge of breaking. "I wanted to pay him, and he wouldn't let me. He said, 'Any work I do after sundown I do because I want to.' "

She smiled at me and laughed, wiping at her black eyeliner roughly with the back of her hand. I laughed with her, still trying to place this Italian-American sweetheart. I know Long Island, I have Irish Catholic cousins who all went to Sacred Heart, and not one of them has ended up dressed like a punk in the middle of Baker, Oregon. Maybe that's why I like her so much.

Before we left town, Angela wrote the mechanic a note on Jan's Italian stationery, put it in an envelope with a piece of pink stone from Brazil, and addressed it to "The Garage Angel." Nobody was there, so we slipped it under the door and drove out of town with the last of the light.

CHAPTER 2

ANGELA AND I woke up to see that we had pitched our tents next to three enormous rolls of rusted barbed wire.

"Welcome to Dachau," Angela said as I unzipped my tent. She was already up, sitting cross-legged in front of her tent, smoking a cigarette. The field looked like a little tent ghetto, with Bedouins of the twentieth century wrapped in brightly colored ripstop nylon. I figured that The Scenicruiser, a vintage Greyhound bus which is the Karamazovs' year-round touring vehicle and serves as a Chautauqua caravan in the summer, must have arrived during the night. I lay half out of my tent, panting in the cool air.

The sky had been soaring from black into blue when

we arrived last night. Angela and I had lost Artis the Spoonman, Jan, and The Nimbus when we hit Boise. Blasting Springsteen on the car speakers at four in the morning, we had wound up at a Seven-Eleven drinking bad coffee with instant cocoa mixed into it, to stay awake. Seven-Elevens are the only all-night establishments in the small towns and cities of the West, and the local hoods tend to congregate there at night. They look quite suburban in the fluorescent light, underage kids sipping Slurpies spiked with vodka. We asked for directions to Rosalie Sorel's place. She had offered her homestead near Boise as a gathering place for the Chautauqua, to get the show together before the first performance. Rosalie is a well-known folksinger, to those who know folksingers. No one at the Seven-Eleven had ever heard of her. It was strictly heavy metal behind the Slurpie machine, and the hoods stared at us dumbly. Wired on sugar, we headed out of town with the crumpled Xerox map someone had handed to Angela at the Country Fair.

An hour later, down a gravel road that felt as if it must be leading us in a huge circle back to the Seven-Eleven, someone was waiting with a candle lantern, marking the entrance to Rosalie's place. At the time it seemed both normal and supernatural that a stranger would be waiting up all night for the Chautauqua to arrive, a hooded face I could not remember in the morning.

Now my body hurt all over from the endless driving, and I wondered how long I had slept. People were starting to throw open their tent flaps and move around the field purposefully, carrying toothbrushes and towels. I moved farther back into my tent. I didn't want to be there. I didn't know where to brush my teeth, and it suddenly felt as if I never would. Most of the Chautauquans were strangers with whom I had talked in the way my generation has, of being familiar without ever introducing ourselves by name, so that as time goes by it becomes more and more embarrassing to make the simple exchange. I always start by assuming that we have been introduced, that they remember my name but I can't remember theirs, and these half-conversations start up while the subtext—What is your name?—becomes so overwhelming that I can hardly bear to continue the conversation. What is this need to name? The contemporary view that if a fear can be named, it can also be tamed or transformed, is all about control really. All a name can ultimately bestow is recognition.

The sound of someone banging on a pot pulled me out of my tent.

"That must be breakfast."

Angela and I joined the general drift of people coming from the fields. There seemed to be about forty of us, not counting the pack of small children. A large group had gathered around the coffee. There was a stove and a rough kitchen set up on Rosalie's back patio, and a huge bowl of fruit and yogurt into which someone was dipping an enormous ladle. I had been instructed to bring a bowl and a spoon on this trip, so I got my portion of yogurt and sat down quietly, too shy to stand in the coffee line. The day was warming up, and sitting barelegged on the flagstones felt like summer to me, a hundred summers on verandahs in New England near the beaches of my childhood, on the other side of the earth.

Dmitri walked up and handed me a cup of coffee out of nowhere and sat next to me, careful not to touch. I had been looking for him all along. Not wanting to, but unable to stop. We had been together by the banks of the Long Tom River at the Country Fair two days ago, and his body was still imprinted on mine; somehow he had left his shadow behind. We had avoided each other since, for his girlfriend had been at the Fair, and she could sense my echo all around him. She was not coming on Chautauqua. She had been with Dmitri for six months and had immediately moved into the enormous bed-and-breakfast inn the Karamazovs owned and begun to work as their innkeeper. It was all very West Coast, these lightning-quick life choices.

Dmitri lived on the top floor of the inn. The other Karamazovs had bought their own houses several years before, after a brief experiment in trying to live together even when not on tour. The girlfriend had gone back to the inn after the Country Fair to keep the business going and wait, I supposed, for the other shoe to fall. She knew about us. I really had nothing against her, and in other circumstances we might have become friends; but I didn't know her, and I didn't want to, for there were no promises I could make to her. Dmitri and I had been meeting in coffee shops, in doorways, and at the edge of stages for years. He has a thick rope of black hair which he wears in a braid, and a wide back to dream against. He moves through life with a recklessness that draws people to him.

Last year at the Fair I had asked him, only half joking, if we were ever going to get together. He didn't answer, and when I walked him home late that night to his campsite at The Circus, he had grabbed me suddenly, kissing me over and over again in the shadows of a crafts booth, still saying no. I hadn't known how unhappy he was. This summer at the Fair we had gone to the riverbank after the midnight show, and the crescent moon cut into the pale sky over his shoulder as he spread himself over me on the grass. I laughed myself to sleep that morning when I got back to my tent at dawn—after it was all over, we hadn't been able to find my pants, and I had walked bare-assed through the Fair back to the campsite. Not that anyone noticed. The Fair is the kind of place where nakedness draws no more attention than a giggle, especially when the night has gotten so late that it is almost day again.

As Rosalie's breakfast became a group meeting, I realized that a small bulletin board had been hung from a tree with a schedule for the day tacked onto it. This struck me as funny and reassuring all at once. I waited to see what would happen and wondered who had brought a computer on Chautauqua (Dmitri, as it turned out). Dmitri and I sat next to each other as if there were no invisible boundary crossed now, recrossed again. We hardly spoke. Committees were formed to handle the stage set-up and tear-down, food, the educational workshops, child care, even the recycling of garbage (that this was accomplished while traveling every day for miles in ancient vehicles still stuns me). Dmitri and Rebo Flordigan seemed to be the leaders, Dmitri handling the bookings and performance-oriented concerns, while Rebo covered the larger, logistical end of things. Rebo is a tall blonde from Minnesota, with a wide, gentle, Scandinavian face. Though she and Dmitri have been divorced for years, they continue the Chautauqua together every summer. She carries her heart close to the surface, and when she sings, her voice shimmers through the air. She was in love with another Chautauquan, a drummer named Max, who sprang about like a young lion, working under the trucks, on top of the stage rigging, playing with the children.

After the meeting I consulted with Allen, my trapeze rigger. He would be the one to decide how to keep the twenty-two-foot poles he had cut for my trapeze rig up in the air, where to place the rig in relation to the stage, and how to stake it out. We would have to dig foot-and-a-half-deep holes for the poles to rest in wherever we set up. At the top of the poles, a metal brace would be bolted together, forming a crosspiece. My trapeze bar would finally hang about fifteen feet above the ground. I had sent Allen some rough drawings before the tour, and he had ordered the crosspiece from a machinist. The trees he had cut from his own land near the Oregon coast. We still didn't know if it would work, but Dmitri swore by Allen's rigging abilities. The summer before, he had rigged a wire from telephone poles and trees to the stage to allow an actress to glide through midair suspended in a harness while singing an aria.

Allen was a slow speaker, and I felt nervous about getting the rig up in time for me to practice on it before the first show. But I could tell he was not the kind who could be hurried. He smoked a lot of dope and was rumored to live off family money. Over the summer I found out that Dmitri was right; he was also a fantastic rigger.

There was not going to be a net, that was certain. The type of act I do is traditionally performed without a net. It is a controlled, slow, balletic act performed on a single bar, with no flying from bar to bar. There are backward falls off the bar in which I catch myself at the last moment with my feet, and turns that look impossible. If I missed with a hand or a foot at those moments, I could certainly be killed, or paralyzed, which is exactly why people come to see the act in the first place. Real, undeniable danger is what makes circus interesting to most people. The physical feats, the big cats and the trainer in the ring are not dependent on "tricks." The appeal is simply the performers' ability to remain utterly concentrated in front of a crowd. The feeling of a circus audience watching a very dangerous act is like a crowd in the street watching a building go up in flames: horror mixed with a certain satisfaction. Of course, it takes the same ability to be an actor. But if an actor's concentration slips, at worst he is panned by the critics or fired by the director: but he does not generally end up maimed or dead.

The trapeze bar provided physical clarity that had been absent from the rest of my creative life. In writing, acting, everything I had spent my life doing up to this point, there was ego peeking over my shoulder and questioning each sentence that spilled off the hand or the lips. There were moments of transcendence that made it at least possible to continue, but trapeze has the same clarity of existence as the weather. There is no time for self-doubt, there is only the rhythm of the breathing, the swing of the body up onto the bar, and the taut, heartbreaking moment of balance.

In the afternoon, a light rain began to fall, the almost mist of the Northwest which greens everything it touches. In the mountains of Idaho you can get the feeling that if you stood in one place for long enough, it would grow up all around you. Mosses and ferns and long creeping vines of green and yellow would entwine themselves around your body until no one could tell where your legs had once begun. I crawled back into my tent and slept. It had been days since I had gotten any real sleep; the Country Fair took days to recover from. Allen had promised to hang my trapeze somewhere by tomorrow, even if just from the trees.

I had gone to my first Country Fair at eighteen, just a few weeks after I first met Dmitri, two years before Rosalita and I went to Paris. I came to the Fair that summer with Rosalita, as part of the Alligator Revue. The troupe included ourselves, Samwise the juggler, and Mazuba the Magician, as well as Reverend Chumleigh and Brodie. The stage Chumleigh brought us to at the Fair was The Circus, though at that point it was called "Chumleighland" in honor of the Reverend, who was one of the headlining acts, along with the Karamazovs. A few years later it was changed to "Not Chumleighland" after there was a falling out between the Karamazovs and the Reverend. I never quite understood, or wanted to understand, the story behind the break, but the stage was eventually renamed The Circus, a fairly neutral choice considering the egos involved. Rosalita and

I performed our brief turn on the stage with the other vaudevillians, sweating in our ridiculously heavy costumes—red velvet Shriners' costumes we had bought second-hand, which looked wonderful and felt terrible. They were totally impractical for a pair of acrobats because their wide, baggy pants made it very difficult to grab hold of each other as much as we needed to during the act, but we looked great in them, and we wouldn't give them up. We ended our act by falling straight out into the audience from a two-high shoulder stand; Rosalita perched on my shoulders until she fell into the arms of a waiting Karamazov Brother. Dmitri and I flirted all weekend, until he knocked a tooth out juggling baseball bats.

Rosalita made her way into the arms of another Karamazov, Alyosha, and they made love one night on a bunk inside Mr. Big, the gray school bus that was the Karamazov tour bus in the old days. I pretended to sleep on a nearby bunk and pushed my ears shut while I longed for Dmitri. One year I sent him a string of rosebuds and bells; another year he tried to seduce me on the doorstep of a brownstone in New York City.

For a few years I stopped going to the Country Fair. These were the cement summers. I stayed in New York, living in a humid East Village apartment with a man who lied to me over and over again until he finally told me the truth and left. It was four years before I could come back to the Fair and remember everything I had forgotten about during those long summers of restaurant jobs and no theatre work to speak of. Adults dressing up in homemade costumes and dancing in the parade for three days seemed no more absurd than life in New York had become for me. It took more energy to step over the bodies in the street than it used to, and I was always running out of spare change.

. . .

The pot was being banged again over at Rosalie's. It sounded close. The little field was quiet in the late afternoon, and a baby was crying somewhere near the stream that ran down past the house. There was a show meeting scheduled for after dinner, and the performers pulled chairs in a circle around Dmitri. There were only about ten of us, since the band didn't have to be there. Angela was in the band, and every time I watched her I wished I could play saxophone. The band always had fun on Chautauqua. All of the performers except me had been on the tour before. Faith Petric had been performing all over the country for years and was an old friend of Rosalie's. I had seen her every year on The Circus stage at the Fair. My favorite number was her song about being a dog. She would lead everyone in a verse of panting, the audience sitting happily with their tongues hanging out like a pack of hounds.

Then there was Artis the Spoonman, who was hard to keep up with, and Toes Tiranoff, a tap dancer from New York who said nothing and listened with a bemused expression as the others discussed the show. Magical Mystical Michael, a blond hippie with a heavy Bronx accent who seemed incredibly naive onstage while pulling off wonderfully smooth sleight-of-hand tricks, would close the first act. This year the climax of his act was the levitation of a brave volunteer from the audience. I still hadn't figured it out, though I thought it had something to do with the magic box the volunteer lay down on top of. But then, I make it a point never to watch a magic act from backstage. I'd rather be fooled.

That was the first half of the show. There would be a ten-minute intermission, and then I was slated to begin the second half. Hearing the show order all laid out like that made it seem to be happening soon. In reality, we had five days before the first show in Boise. I wondered about practicing my act from a bar hung from the trees and whether the band would have learned my music by then. After my act came Sandy Bradley, a singer and comedienne who hosts a radio show on National Public Radio out of Seattle. She would croon a sardonic love song in a cafe setting with the band backing her up.

Dmitri and Magical Mystical Michael decided to do a reworked version of a two-man straitjacket escape act as a filler. Rebo and Jan's musical duo would be next. Last of all, which means top billing, would be the Karamazovs. No one asked what they would be doing. They never rehearsed for the Chautauqua. It was the closest thing to vacation time for them, and they always put something together at the last minute.

After reading off the show order, Dmitri looked around at us.

"So, what do you think of scrapping the whole idea of a vaudeville revue and writing a play?"

Silence.

"Dmitri, people don't like plays as much as variety

shows." Rebo sounded as if she had been through this conversation a million times before.

"*We* don't like them as much, you mean." Artis always cut through the bullshit.

"Have you got one written?"

"We could all write one together, starting tonight."

First everyone was against the idea, then a few people started to come around to it. An hour later it was decided to stick to the original decision: vaudeville revue. A typical Chautauquan process. What struck me was that these people actually seemed to listen to each other. That hardly ever happens in the theatre, or anywhere else. Dmitri was not too happy with the outcome; he was bored with vaudeville revues. But most performers want to do revues, at least partly because they need hardly any rehearsal, since everyone has his or her own act down solid. Also, a play is not as surefire, and some performers don't feel comfortable outside of the one character they have developed for their act. Another bottom line is that since no one gets paid to do the Chautauqua, they want to do what is easiest and leave some free time for what they see as vaudeville summer camp.

As people wandered off, Dmitri asked me to go for a walk. We started up the streambed that went past the house and farther into the mountains. The big rocks next to the stream were perfect for jumping; there was no moon, and the stars were coming out clear and white in the hard mountain air. We leapt from rock to rock, following each other as if it were a dare set by children. I started heading away from the stream up toward the cliff. The stones became boulders and jagged plateaus away from the stream. In the dark it was hard to tell how high we were climbing, and the base of the cliff looked closer than it really was.

One more step, and we were there, at the bottom of the cliff, with nowhere left to go. Dmitri was very close, and looking past him I saw the stones shining against the stream which flowed black and smooth, far away. Neither of us spoke of the present, of the woman he had left at his house who hated me without knowing me, and who could blame her. It had become the time to say yes. No is familiar to me; it is a word that mortals use. Yes is from the angels. He lifted me up and kissed me against the cliffside. We made love, feet slipping on the ledge as I pushed against him; I don't know how he kept us balanced with the sharp edges of the stone pressing their teeth into me until I couldn't feel them anymore as I came down on top of him and he grabbed at the rocks above me. Something held us up against the ledge, for we were nowhere, past valley and cliff and black stones. As if being in love could be a place like anywhere else on the map.

CHAPTER
3

A DROP OF WATER landing on my right eyelid woke me up. The light was pearly through the walls of Dmitri's tent, and all of our heat had condensed into salty drops, which hung, pendulous, from the nylon roof. There was a strange residue of breath and sweat. The water ran down my cheek into my mouth, and I thought: I am tasting him again. Dmitri was awake, but his eyes were closed. I couldn't remember when it was last night that my arms had simply let go of his. Did he watch me fall away from him before sleeping? His hand lay open and heavy on my breast, and I covered it with mine. The middle finger of his left hand was missing the last section of a digit, an accident from his childhood; while showing his brother the spinning wheel of a bicycle, he had stuck his finger into the whirring metal magic.

A recognizable mark, I thought, if he were ever killed. I always have my darkest thoughts on awakening, when I am overwhelmed by the distance between having to do and having done, and by a terrible certainty that what has been given will be taken away. Dmitri turned to me and opened his eyes. All I could think of to say was good morning. He held me and whispered sweetness into my ears, words that filled me up like apples and honey.

The light was hardening into day, and I wanted to make it from his tent to mine before the whole camp was awake. I wasn't ready to go public yet. The grass was tall and wet outside his tent, and I walked back trailing my hands in it, soaking myself up to the thighs. It was a good, strong cold from the dew. I crawled into my sleeping bag, glad to be surrounded by my own belongings. I waited for the breakfast bell, hand over my breast as his had been, to keep myself company.

The Circle was set for eleven o'clock. I wondered what a circle was and worried that it was going to go on and on, involving a lot of hand-holding. Yesterday a huge yurt had been set up, and we were to gather there this morning. The nomadic Mongolian dwelling is round, with white canvas stretched over walls made out of wooden slats that fold like an accordion and are quite high. It is an enormous job to raise. Across the top of the walls is a guy wire, with more wooden slats attached, holding up the circle that forms the peak of the conical roof, also covered with canvas. The tension of the slats and the design itself hold up the roof; there are no bolts or nails. It takes about ten people to raise it. Ivan Karamazov was the "yurt captain," shouting out orders and directing traffic. It generally takes our Chautauqua yurt crew about an hour to raise or dismantle a yurt, but Ivan insists that the Mongolians do it in no time flat. There is no response to that. I suppose we have to take his word for it while feeling slightly guilty at not, in the end, *being* Mongolian.

The Chautauqua has two yurts, a small one and a larger one, twenty and forty feet in diameter respectively. They are set up at performances as the space for the afternoon workshops. Because of the light filtering through the canvas and the grass underfoot, they feel very open, yet forty or more people can sit against the walls of the big yurt and leave a space in the middle. Which is exactly what we did for the Circle.

Dmitri had saved a spot for me next to him. It was all very tribal suddenly, and I recoiled from the symbolism of it. The new woman sitting next to a tribal leader with everyone watching. I was very quiet. Susan, a beautiful Asian woman in her thirties, began the Circle. She was, I realized, in many ways the spiritual guardian of the Chautauqua. We all said our names, why we had come, and what we thought we would get out of being on Chautauqua. Some answers were long and complicated, more than I really wanted to know. I had no personal agenda I wanted to share in a situation like this; when my turn came, I kept it brief.

Susan put a big shopping bag in the middle and told everyone to go up and take one of whatever was inside.

This broke everyone loose from their moorings at the wall, and of course all of the kids ran for the bag, which made us laugh. We each took out a colored pencil, labeled "Chautauqua," and a tiny handkerchief, arranged like a runaway's stick and bundle. Inside the kerchief was a smooth, dark piece of obsidian, a quarter (to call home), and a piece of paper, like a fortune. The paper had one word typed on it. Mine was "Flexibility." I looked around the Circle, knowing that there are no secrets in any tribe, and not everyone was pleased to see me with Dmitri. Dr. Dennis, a Harvard-trained psychiatrist who is also a Chautauquan, tried to explain to me later in the trip that by being with Dmitri I was "sitting very close to the flame" of the group. "Flexibility," I thought, for the trapeze, to hang and drop and spin; arching back on the bar before the drop to the ankles which always hurts. Flexibility, for people who watch what I do when it's nobody's business but my own. . . . Flexibility.

Dmitri took out an eagle feather and a bundle of sage, given to the Chautauqua by the Blackfoot tribe in Montana, whom we would be visiting later in the tour. He lit the sage and held it in front of me, passing the smoky bundle up and down while fanning it at me with the feather. I found out later it is a Native American cleansing ritual called "smudging." I didn't know how to react, partly wanting to laugh, but enjoying it. After a few moments Dmitri handed the sage to me and gestured that I should do the same to the person next to me, Artis the Spoonman. There was no explanation, so I just stumbled along, waving the sage over Artis and feeling like an idiot, wondering how long I should keep it up. There was something very intimate about the process, and the burning sage smelled dry and sweet, like the desert. Eventually Artis opened his eyes, and I stopped. He smiled at me and took the sage, which was passed quietly around.

Susan produced a Japanese doll, a small wooden figure with two blank eyes, painted white. She explained that this was a journey doll, and we should, as a group, color a design into one eye now, and into the other at the end of Chautauqua. We passed the totem around with an India-ink pen, each adding a line. I wondered how one was to begin a journey with truly blank eyes, no expectations. But maybe that's something that only an inanimate object can do (or perhaps a Mongolian), and I drew a thick black line on the pupil of the doll with envy.

After the meeting, things began to move very fast for the rest of the day. The dress rehearsal was set for the early evening, and some local friends of Rosalie's were coming. By late afternoon we had the trapeze rig up for the first time. The ground was hard and rocky, and Allen and I chipped away at it with a pickax. It was hot, very hot, and the bolts of the crossbar were searing as we tightened them down onto the tall wooden poles that were to support the trapeze. This process took a long time because the bolts had to be tightened down evenly on all sides, and since the poles were actually freshly cut trees, they were uneven in diameter. Allen threw ten washers onto one bolt and twenty onto the next. There was never any established order to it, since the weather also affected the width of the trees, so each time we put it together the bolts were guess-work.

Twenty-one feet doesn't sound high until you are stand-ing beneath the rig, when it looks very far away. To raise it we used a truck, pulling up on the crossbar while four people manned each pole and walked the trapeze into place. Then the guy wires were tightened down from where they had been staked out with a "come-along," a pulley-and-lever system that could adjust the tension. When the frame was perpendicular to the ground we shoveled dirt back into the holes and patted them down. It was definitely a homemade job. Professional rigs are made of hollow aluminum sections that fit together and have feet of steel piping, halved, onto which the rig can roll up before being staked down in the same manner we used. In both cases, the tension of the guy wires keeps the rig in place. Our Chautauqua version was simply more difficult to raise and put together because wooden poles are impossibly heavy and there was a multitude of bolts that needed to be tight-ened every time. But now it was up, and it was strong.

The stage crew had set up the stage next to the trapeze; it folded down from the side of the old wooden trailer we dragged around with us. The Chautauqua had bought the trailer years ago. It was made of plywood painted blue, and it looked as if it would rattle to pieces if it were pulled at highway speed. However, the truck that pulled the trailer couldn't make highway speed anyway. The side of the trailer folded down, and a proscenium with a roll-bar back-drop was set up where the wall of the trailer had been.

The backdrop was a pastoral scene of a country road wind-ing off into the distance, and two painted wooden trees were set up on either side, framing the picture. The stage was braced from underneath with portable iron legs, and once the backdrop was up, the inside of the trailer became the backstage and dressing room. The lights were rigged from a small metal frame fitted into place above the stage, and a spotlight was set up on top of The Rubber Chicken, which was parked opposite the stage. Two generators were set up in the woods to power the lighting system.

No one knew exactly when the show would begin; there was so much more to do before we would be ready. I ran to jump into the river after sweating all day. My arms ached from swinging the pickax. I am not a large person—five feet, four inches, one hundred and ten pounds—but I was in good condition, having trained hard all spring for my act. Still, swinging a pickax in the blazing heat for even a very short time is more than most people my size would willingly attempt. Lying on my belly in the freezing water, I tried to remember everything my trapeze teacher had ever told me: warm up well, especially the back and the arms; stay warmed up until you go on. Never become overcon-fident or you will fall. Falling was something I tried not to think about. Superstitious, I pushed it from my mind.

Dmitri would be spotting me that night (keeping close to me during the act, to try to catch me if I fell). But I knew that the chances of his actually catching me were pretty slim. I simply couldn't fall.

As the director of the show and a member of the band, Dmitri had been running back and forth all day from the show site to the band rehearsal, and we had hardly seen each other. After my swim I went to look for him, since he wanted to come with me to practice for the evening show. I hadn't been up on the bar in five days, because of the Fair, and it felt like a long time. There was no way to hang my bar lower for practice, and I wasn't going to risk it without a spotter. Swinging up to sit on the bar, I looked everywhere but down, and suddenly I didn't want to do trapeze anymore. It was strange, being up that high. I had grown used to practicing at a lower level. The routine is the same, of course, but it takes a lot more nerve the higher up you go.

I forced myself to go through the routine, each move a force of will. Dmitri stayed with me, and as I sat balanced, poised to fall into my first ankle drop, I hesitated and told him how scared I was. I went ahead anyway, gasping when I hit the bar with my feet—not from the pain, from the fear. I wished that no one was coming to watch tonight, and I was embarrassed to be so afraid in front of Dmitri; but I had no choice. I made it through the routine very slowly, psyching myself up before each move. I had wanted to impress him, though he had seen the routine before, in Seattle; but now the bar was hung higher, and the show was tonight.

When I got down, I was ashamed and abrupt with him, ready for him to walk away. He asked me to go swimming instead. We went back to the river and stripped noncha-lantly, as if it were nothing. I moved quickly and kept myself from looking at him. There was the sound of the children playing upstream. Shy of his seeing my body in the daylight, I floated belly down, my hands walking over the smooth rocks. Looking down through the clear water, I saw huge telephone poles scattered up and down the river, half submerged.

"Where did all those telephone poles come from?" I asked. "Did there used to be a road here?"

He looked at me to see if I was joking. I stared back. Then he started laughing. His whole face laughed, mouth open, eyes crushed together at the corners, big bushy eyebrows bouncing up and down.

"Those aren't telephone poles! They're trees, regular trees." He tried to breathe. "This is where telephone poles come from."

Angela and I made dinner together that night. Spaghetti for fifty people, with every available vegetable thrown into the sauce. We played the Pretenders very loud out of the doors of The Rubber Chicken and made our way around the kitchen. All of the seats had been taken out of the bus and replaced by a full-size refrigerator, a propane cook stove, and counter space with drawers. Angela was tired of losing all of her crushes to men, she told me with a bit of an edge. I said nothing. She was trying not to sulk. The band had rehearsed all afternoon, and no one really felt ready for a show tonight. We danced to rock-and-roll in the bus and threw the spaghetti onto the ceiling to see if it was done. I felt safe with Angela, not knowing whether or not to avoid the other women, all of whom knew Dmitri and none of whom knew me.

"My specialty is picking women that I can't have,"

Angela said, sampling the sauce and making a face. "I used to have a crush on Rebo."

"You and Dmitri have the same taste," I commented, thinking how different Rebo and I are: she, tall and midwestern; me, small, sharp-boned, and urban.

"He's starting to think I want to steal all of his girlfriends." She gave me a look. "He's right, of course."

"I'm not his girlfriend."

"Then you're available?"

I laughed. "No."

"What about her?"

"Who?"

"His girlfriend."

"I don't know. He says he'll call her. She knows already, of course."

"Do you think he will call her?"

"I don't know."

That was a lie. I did think he would call. I just didn't know what he would say. My stomach clenched, and I changed the subject. The shadows of the mountains were dropping in on us quickly. It was nearly six o'clock. Everyone looked harried as they arrived and gulped down the pasta. No one wanted to do a show that night.

The show began an hour late, but the audience was small and just as happy to watch us prepare. The temperature had dropped, as it always does in the mountains, and I pulled on a layer of tights, sweatshirt, and leg warmers. Above us the sky was still light, but you had to look straight up to see it. There were two sunsets here: the

moment the light stopped touching the valley, and the
moment it left the sky for good. Trying to stretch and keep
moving, I stayed behind the trailer, which had become a
backstage like any other, only smaller. People were changing into costumes and passing back and forth a list with
the order of the acts. Faith opened the show with a story
of seeing the Chautauquas that came to her town when she
was a child. She described how the family would pack a
picnic and stay at the fairgrounds all day. I didn't have to
go on until the second act, so I pulled my straw mat out
behind the audience and lay with my legs stretched as far
as they would go, always moving, flexing and pointing,
running off the energy somehow.

Faith had a way of making everyone feel welcome,
which was one of the reasons Dmitri liked to open the show
with her. She also surprised you. With her gray hair and
acoustic guitar, she looked like a sweet old lady who was
going to sing camp songs. She did know plenty of cowboy
tunes and would sing them around a campfire. But when
she performed on Chautauqua she went for the humorous
and the political. She probably would have been labeled
a "Commie" in the fifties. She reminded me of the folk
records my mother used to play at home: the Weavers;
Pete Seeger and Joan Baez singing "Joe Hill." A child of
the sixties, I used to beg her to play me that song before
bed every night. Faith was no cliché either; she didn't let
people stay comfortable thinking she was just a sweet old
lady for long. She was angry and funny and very direct.

Toes Tiranoff was also in the first act. A baby-faced
man of medium height, he shuffled onstage looking almost

apologetic and murmured, "Hit it, boys." The band struck up a swing tune, and he started to dance. Toes had studied with the old hoofers in New York—the dancers from Harlem who had nailed bottle caps to their shoes and tapped on the street for change when they were first getting started. When Toes danced, it was as if his face had been stuck onto another body. As he shuffled, tapped, and spun below the neck, his face retained a strangely detached look, as if this were all happening to someone else. It had an eerie overall effect, I thought, but I liked it. How could you not like Toes, for when the song came to an end he stood there, panting slightly, and then took his bow with a flourish of his hat that belied the shy and flustered expression on his face.

After Toes came a musical combo made up of acoustic instruments and several singers. This slot was destined to be somewhat fluid over the tour. In the end it became a gospel chorus conducted by Ivan Karamazov and backing up Cici Dawn, a singer who was going on Chautauqua for the first time. Cici belted out a gospel number that was strong enough to hide the fact that most of the people in the chorus weren't really singers, and the chorus gave a lot of people the chance to get onstage and have some fun singing together. I don't think the audience knew quite what to make of the line of twenty or so people who crammed the stage to back her up, but Cici was great. Anyone who wanted to sing could join the chorus on Chautauqua.

Closing out the first half was Magical Mystical Michael. His act was an expanded version of what he had done at the Fair that year. He would open with some sleight of hand, using handkerchiefs or some other standard magician's trick, just to get the audience's attention, and his big finish was the levitation of a volunteer. What really got the audience's attention, though, was Michael himself. He was very droll, with a teddy bear quality that lent itself well to his innocent demeanor. My favorite moment was when he would turn to the audience, halfway through a trick, and remark in his heavy Bronx accent: "I know what you're thinking—so far, so what?" For the rest of the summer we would all stop in the midst of practically any activity and ask each other: "So far, so what?" But he was smooth, and though I did eventually figure out how he managed to levitate his brave volunteers, most of his sleight of hand was too well done for me to understand the mechanics of it. The thing about magic is that once you know how a trick is done, you can't believe that everyone doesn't see it right away, and I was happy to remain a gullible spectator along with the rest of the audience.

The show was long that first night—much too long—and everyone knew it. The acts were solid, but the transitions were sloppy, and it was getting colder and darker. Nevertheless the audience loved it. They were great, all ten of them. I ran off for one final pee in the woods at intermission. I was afraid of not being able to see the bar in the dark, afraid of the wind, which had risen, making the bar swing.

"Go slow, it doesn't matter," Dmitri said when he came backstage to check in with me, making sure I was ready to go on. I felt as if it were days since we had rehearsed together. I knew it shouldn't matter, a dress rehearsal in the middle of the woods in Idaho for ten neighbors, but it did. It wasn't just them I was thinking of, but the Chautauquans who would be watching me for the first time. I stripped off my sweats and pulled up the white sequined costume, which barely covered my nipples. I had to go on soon or my muscles would get cold. I put chalk on my hands and listened to Magical Mystical Michael's introduction to my act. His slow, Bronx-accented speech sounded like home. I tried to remember to breathe.

Dmitri half squatted into a *plié*, feet planted wide, and I gave him my hands, climbing up easily onto his shoulders. I stood with my knees pressed against the back of his neck. We had found no other way for me to reach the bar, not having another thick rope for me to climb up to it. I put out my arms in a half circle, hands relaxed and palms facing upward. I smiled, and out we came from behind the trailer to make my entrance. The band hadn't learned my music yet. It was an original piece, which Benjamin, the musical director, was busy arranging and transposing. He sat at the foot of one of my poles, for tonight, with a mandolin. It was dark and clear, but the moon wouldn't make it over the ridge until much later, and the trees were outlined in hard white edges of light. I reached my arms up as high as they could go, and Dmitri went up on half toe. I grabbed the bar, still smiling, and the spotlight came on full.

The first half of the routine felt like a dream, or a memory of something I had seen someone else perform. I was operating purely on muscle-memory and adrenaline. The second half was slower and took more control. It felt like work, and I hoped it didn't look like it. I rushed some of the moments, not allowing the audience enough time to applaud. You have to stop very clearly in the circus and acknowledge them in order to give them permission to acknowledge you. Later, I learned to lengthen and enjoy these moments; now I was too scared, thinking only of the moves, trying to remember to breathe and point my toes. The bar was only a thin black line in this light, but I found it by instinct. I was vaguely aware of the mandolin playing below, and of the gasps when I did a series of unexpected moves that had been choreographed to look like a loss of control. I leaned back into the last moment, a back bend onto the bar, which rubbed painfully on my tailbone, letting go of my hands and drawing my legs tight together, toes pointed. I held the moment of balance as long as possible, then shifted, and did my last full fall to the ankles. I pulled myself up to face them, one arm outstretched to blow a kiss, toe to the opposite knee. On the ground again, Dmitri kissed me again and again, neither of us caring who noticed. He knew, he was the only one who knew; I hadn't fallen.

Later that night, after the show came down, Angela and I went into Idaho City with Dmitri and Fyodor, the Karamazov who was silent onstage and alternately grim and charming offstage. Idaho City has wooden sidewalks and one paved street down the middle of town. The only tavern was "Killer's," which had a small herd of motorcycles parked out front. I wanted to go because I was hyper after the show, and because Angela wanted to go. We each ordered a whiskey, and the bartender knew who we were, being a friend of Rosalie's daughter, who worked behind the bar some nights. It was late, and the place was quiet. Angela started to play the jukebox, but I was suddenly exhausted and wanted to leave. Dmitri suggested going to the hot springs nearby for a midnight dip, and I said yes. Angela stayed with Fyodor, ordering another drink with a reckless smile. Fyodor stared back at her, looking not unlike the Big Bad Wolf.

We drove out of town, away from Rosalie's, up higher and higher into the mountains. The hot springs were farther away than he had remembered, and we didn't know if we had enough gas to make it. We watched the gas gauge drop, talking and talking; counting the animals we saw: a badger, a possum, two raccoons. When we saw the elk Dmitri pulled over and rolled down his window.

"Listen."

I heard nothing. Dmitri stayed motionless. From close by, above us on the hill, which rose straight up from the road, a throaty moaning broke out, was cut off, then picked up again, louder.

"It's the elk," he whispered. "A herd of elk."

Their cries were wild and repetitive. I reached for his hand as they moved away through the underbrush, clumsily snapping branches and breaking through rotted logs, not caring if anyone heard them go. They called out to each other in their strange language full of ghosts and lust. We turned around and drove back down to Idaho City and on to Rosalie's, almost out of gas, coasting in neutral.

CHAPTER 4

BOISE, IDAHO, HAS a green lawn for its fairgrounds, and the dirt came up easily in the shovel. Big, chocolaty chunks of earth. There were no big rocks, no surprises. I dug both holes for my trapeze in about fifteen minutes, record time. I laid the top pieces of grass-covered sod carefully aside, so that I could replace them when we were done. I was the one on Chautauqua who made contact with the earth; the raw, absolute nature of it, that is. Not the earth as a metaphor; the earth as an element. Other people had contacts to make when we arrived somewhere: Rebo and Susan met with the presenters and community leaders; Dmitri huddled with the stage and lighting crews and conferred on the site for the stage; and

Fyodor, who always led the parade, met with Susan and Rebo and decided on the route. I met with the dirt, bringing my shovel, pickax, and metal bar. I liked digging because it felt clean. The work was too physically hard to spend much time thinking about it. It was simple, making four walls of smooth dirt which had to stay the same width all the way down. I loved the clarity of the accomplishment when it was finished, and I wanted to find people and drag them over to see the beautiful holes I had dug. It always put me in a good mood to dig.

It was sunny, but not the blistering heat we had been having at Rosalie's. Early that morning we broke camp and loaded up The Scenicruiser and The Rubber Chicken with the kitchen and everyone's camping gear. I took down my tent, which was still set up near Angela's, though I hadn't slept in it since the first night. Angela predicted that it would stay in the storage bays underneath The Scenicruiser for the rest of the trip, but I wasn't so sure.

The truck and the trailer had been driven into Boise the night before, and an early-morning contingent of the stage crew went into town to set up the stage. There wasn't going to be a parade. Ticket sales had been good, and it was decided to skip the parade and spend the time getting the acts together. Dmitri had been changing the order and making cuts ever since our overlong, semi-disastrous dress rehearsal, but only the band had actually rehearsed since then. Tonight would be like running a brand-new show for the first time in front of an audience.

The trapeze rig took several hours to get up; it was only our second time. There were no trees close by, so we had to run a long set of lines to a lone Douglas fir on the far side of the fairgrounds. The other lines were staked out into the dirt at a forty-five-degree angle from the rig. Allen always used trees to tie off the rig when he could; I think he instinctively trusted them more. We used big truck axles as stakes for the wires, which were guyed out into the ground. Allen pounded the stakes in with a sledge hammer, that strange ring of metal on metal that always sounds far away, even if you're right next to it. Allen and I worked well together, I thought, although we moved through life very differently. I always wanted to get going sooner and would have to try hard to remember not to push him too much. Allen could not be rushed, and he always remained infuriatingly unruffled. He had a dietary problem that forced him to prepare all of his meals separately in his van. After his meal he had to smoke a joint as well, but once he started working, he worked hard, and so did I, so we got along.

I knew that he and the other men on Chautauqua who did a lot of the physical labor were watching to see how I would hold up to the stress of putting up and tearing down the rig every day. I couldn't do it alone, but I went about it steadily, without a break, until it was done. I knew they were watching because it was a lot of work, and they were worried that they were going to have to rig the trapeze in addition to their stage crew responsibilities. In the end, all of the work could be done by Allen and me except for the final raising of the rig. Once all of the bolts and bars were in place, we would call over whoever was standing nearby to help with the actual raising. It took four people per pole, with Allen in the truck pulling on the crossbar while we walked the poles up and into the holes we had dug. After the rig was in place, we adjusted the guy wires until it was perfectly perpendicular and then tied down the "come-alongs" (metal pulley systems) and marked them with fluorescent tape so that no one would walk into them and no one could loosen them.

It was starting to feel like a festival. The bus was parked next to the fairgrounds, and someone had made sandwiches and drinks for all of us. We didn't have our official cook yet, so we were winging it. Sam, the rotund, bearded kitchen wizard from Eugene, Oregon, wasn't able to come as planned, and Alex, the young woman who was to fill in for him, hadn't yet arrived. The food was always wonderful on Chautauqua, that is, if you like health food and vege-tarian dishes. It was also wonderful because we were sleep-ing outside and working very hard. The best thing about the food was that there was always plenty of it; some people complained about gaining weight on Chautauqua because there was so much food. Also, I had grown so used to living alone that the appearance of a good meal prepared by someone else and not in a restaurant was still a shock to me.

I stayed away from Dmitri at lunch. Ivan, his partner, who with Dmitri was one of the original Karamazovs, was morally outraged at Dmitri because of me, and I was duck-ing his anger. Ivan and his wife were good friends of Dmi-tri's girlfriend at home and were angry partly because of his betrayal of her, and partly because any instability on the part of one of the four Karamazov Brothers was a threat to the whole group. Ivan had walked out on a band rehearsal the day before, furious at Dmitri, who had followed him while everyone else kept a safe distance. The two of them had so much history that people thought that they would make it through this one, too, but it was no secret in the community. A few of the women in the group had come up to me for quiet talks about how unstable Dmitri was, how he would break my heart, and I should steer clear. He had hurt Rebo when they divorced, and now he was doing the same thing to another woman, who was by all reports just as kind and loving as Rebo. I didn't know if they really had my interests at heart or if they were just afraid I was rocking the boat. It was a strange way to meet people for the first time. They assumed a kind of intimacy with Dmitri and me that pissed me off. On the other hand, I liked these women. They were smart, caring, passionate people, and I wanted to be their friend. Beyond this, I had never encountered such a united front of unsolicited advice about a man before. It scared me. So did Ivan's anger. I started to avoid him and his wife, who were longtime acquaintances of mine.

I was also beginning to wonder if the "togetherness" of Chautauqua was only skin deep. Just like the rest of the world, it all depended on whom you were talking to as to how much like a member of a family you felt. Only Chautauqua had pretensions of being different, and I was waiting to see what would come of it. I grabbed my sandwich and hung out near Allen to make it look as if we were talking shop. Dmitri was overwhelmed by getting the first show together, so my strategy probably went unnoticed, but it made me feel better. I tried to think only about the show.

The yurts had been set up early in the morning, and after lunch the people leading the workshops rushed off to begin them. There was no way to keep people out of the yurts until the scheduled time, and it probably didn't matter anyway. People were too curious about what might be inside the strange-looking white tents, and by the time the workshop leader appeared, the yurts were often occupied by people resting, changing babies, eating a picnic lunch. Provide a structure, and it will be filled.

I poked my head into a couple of the yurts but couldn't sit still for very long; I was too preoccupied. In one yurt Faith Petric was leading a song swap. She was quite well known on the folk circuit in Boise and had a circle of fans and local musicians around her. Ivan's wife, Zoe, and her friend Orbit had taken a big bag of juggling clubs out in the middle of the field, and a crowd of people was throwing and dropping clubs wildly and having a great time. Geoffrey and Sylvia, who were in charge of recycling, had set up an environmental display which had, incredibly, a Macintosh computer running on solar energy. I wondered if you could use the computer in the winter, when it rains all the time. Geoffrey explained to me several times how it worked, but I was never able to retain much of what he said.

Angela came from behind while I was talking to Geoffrey.

"What's up?"

I jumped. I couldn't help it. I was edgy.

"Jesus, Angela. You scared me."

She smiled. "Sorry. Do you want to go over to the dorms?"

"Dorms?"

"We're staying in these college dorms, remember? Just for tonight. Everyone's already been over there to sign up. I figured you were still working on the trapeze."

"No. I forgot about the dorms, I guess. Where are they?"

"I'll go over with you. Listen, these dorms have laundry rooms. Everybody's been washing clothes like crazy."

Washing clothes! Clean clothes. Clean underwear. Clean socks. Clean enough to plunge your nose into. It had been a really long time. The dorms were close to the fairgrounds, modern and bricked, with lots of unlocked, expensive bicycles out front. Angela showed me where the Chautauqua was staying. I gave my name to the guard downstairs and was handed a key.

"All singles," Angela whispered, "but we're on the same floor."

"You and me?"

"And Dmitri."

"You want to have a three way, don't you, Angela." I started laughing. She grinned at me. It was becoming part of our daily banter.

"You know I do. Always. Just get rid of that guy with the big nose." Dmitri's profile, with a big nose and Groucho mustache, was constantly ridiculed, on and off stage.

I lugged my backpack up the stairs. My room was a cement cell looking out at the green quadrangle of the school. I could see some Chautauquans playing hackysack on the lawn. They looked like college students, only less conservative. The bed was a single, and the bathroom was down the hall. It had several showers, and for Chautauqua purposes I was sure it was unisex. There was a desk in the room near the window, but it faced the wall. Modern dormitories are the same everywhere. The cement brick walls are painted white on the inside, and all the furniture comes from the same place. Cheap blond wood. I shut the door, sat down at the desk, and stared at the wall.

I had lasted only one year in boarding school. By the time it ended, I was on probation and failing math. They told me that if I pulled my grade up I would be "invited back" (my math grade had fallen from B+ to F in one semester; they suspected that I had a bad attitude). Whatever else I knew, I was certain that I didn't want to be "invited back," so for the final exam I filled my blue book with doodles of butterflies for two hours.

I never should have gone away to school. I was fairly happy—considering that I was fifteen and basically hated anybody telling me what to do—at the school I had been going to since kindergarten. Life at home wasn't that bad either. If I had a fight with my mother, I would move in with my father for a couple of weeks. When that stopped working, it was back to my mother's apartment. Neither of them demanded much more than that I be home by midnight, and it was easy to stay with friends whose parents were even more often absent or more unconcerned than mine were. My parents knew that I smoked pot and probably knew that I was no longer a virgin, but it didn't seem to be a big concern for them. This was the mid-seventies, and many of my friends' parents were too busy experimenting with sex and drugs themselves to pay a whole lot of attention to what their teenagers were doing.

As soon as I got to boarding school, the rules changed. Drugs, of course, were totally forbidden, so I started doing much more of them. If you wanted to have a boy visit you in your room, you signed him in between 6:00 and 8:00 P.M., kept the door open, and kept "three feet on the floor." To me, it seemed totally archaic. When I was fourteen, my mother had taken my boyfriend and me on a trip to Montreal and booked us our own hotel room. To abide by the rules of a patrician New England boarding school (which was never really a serious consideration for me) was to participate in some huge charade. At fifteen I had just read *The Catcher in the Rye* and was as passionate about phoniness as Holden Caulfield was.

I nevertheless made some good friends at boarding school, and we broke all the rules together. It was such a feeling of "us" and "them" that we became totally bonded in adversity. I remember feeling that if it weren't for the friends I had made, I would have had a breakdown, and I think a lot of us felt that way at different times. We were the only ones who could understand each other in the adolescent code of survival outside the law. We would run across the lawns at night, hiding behind hedges from the security cars that patrolled the campus, large and manicured as any college's. We climbed up and down fire escapes in the middle of the night to see our boyfriends or sneak them into our rooms. I looked on it as a sort of well-kept prison camp and couldn't wait to get back to New York.

I lived, of course, in an all-girl dormitory. Across the hall were two roommates, who lay on top of their beds naked, smoking cigarettes out the window all afternoon. Every now and then one would go down to the piano in the common room and sing melancholy songs in her strong, deep voice. I was sure that they were lovers, but years later I found out that they had never actually been together. They always impressed and slightly intimidated me. One was tall, with long dark curls, while the other was lithe and blond, like a twenties movie star.

Down the hall was an English-looking beauty, whose perfect skin and figure we were all jealous of. This was Gwen, who became my best friend that year. We have never been far apart since. She is the friend I hitchhiked across the country to Seattle with that summer after high school. We ended up living in Seattle and Europe together; the "Queen" of the vaudeville troupe we began in Paris. She is the only one of my friends who shares a knowledge of all of my worlds: the two coasts, the Latin classes, and the street performing. Now she is married, the mother of two girls, and living in New York. The girls will probably end up going to the same all-girl private school that we went to, bringing everything full circle. Her marriage and motherhood have made our paths diverge a bit, at least for now. I envy her the noisy companionship of her young family, while she watches me strike out on the road alone again. It's been years since we took a journey together, and it used to be what we did best. When my heart is breaking, I go to her, for she knows my landscape better than anyone.

Before the school year was over, Gwen had been expelled for a variety of misdemeanors, which culminated in her being caught in bed with her boyfriend on a weekend visit to the campus when she was already suspended. Her being kicked out had a lot to do with my failing math. She was a year ahead of me and very good at math. I was terrible with numbers and convinced that I always would be (I always have been). She had already taken the math course that I was having trouble with at the beginning of the year, so we convinced my father to pay her forty dollars a month to "tutor" me. This meant that we could buy an ounce of pot every month, and before every math test she would cram my brain with everything that I needed to know. My grades immediately improved, so my father was happy, and Gwen and I could get stoned for the rest of the month. But by spring term she had left, I was on probation, and most of our friends would either graduate or be thrown out by the end of the year.

. . .

"Still staring at the walls?"

Dmitri stood in the doorway, hair undone and dripping wet from a shower. I had never seen so much hair—long black curls hung down almost to the middle of his back. He saw me staring and shook it like a dog, spraying water on the floor.

"You've never seen The Hair before?"

"Jesus, no!" I laughed. "Do you let it out much?"

"No, I can't let it out or it will take over. It's got to be watched every minute."

Silence. For a minute too long as my laughter faded away.

"Can I come in?"

"Of course."

A strange politeness descended. I felt suddenly as if I didn't know how to act around this man. Perhaps because I was fully dressed and he was naked except for a towel.

"Which room are you in?" I asked.

"Two-oh-six. Down the hall." He paused. "I didn't know what you wanted to do. I mean, the rooms were arranged a long time ago."

"Right. No, it's okay."

"Oh, it's okay, is it? Thanks a lot!" He teased me with a wounded look. I was letting him in, and he knew it. "I haven't seen you all day."

He smelled like fresh water when he got close. We kissed with our eyes open until it was too much for me and I broke away, giving him my throat like a submissive animal. I could stay here forever, I thought, feeling his breath on my skin.

"Don't you guys ever stop to breathe?" Angela was standing in the doorway with a bag of dirty clothes.

"Angela." Dmitri pulled the towel closer around his waist. He always spoke to her like an elder brother, though she was actually a year older than he. I said nothing. Why did I feel guilty?

"Doing laundry? If we don't do it today, we won't get another chance until Montana."

"That sounds like a road sign," I said. "LAST LAUNDRY UNTIL MONTANA." I didn't get up.

"Well, the laundry is in the basement," Angela said, "and I've got soap if you need it."

"Okay." I smiled at her. She was letting me off the hook. She walked off down the hallway, laundry held high on her hip like a child.

"Are you going to do laundry?" I asked Dmitri, and with that one question we were domesticated. Yes, he wanted to, of course, but he didn't have time. He had to be back at the fairgrounds earlier than anybody else. I would do it. No, I *wanted* to. The thing is, I really *did* want to do it. To take care of him somehow. Later, doing the laundry, I felt as if I were conjuring. Mixing our clothes together and then dividing them into a whites and a coloreds wash, it was as if I were forging us into a couple, almost unconsciously. It had been a long time since I had washed a man's clothes. I struggled with folding the button-down shirts and did a lousy job, as always. I don't wear button-down shirts, and he doesn't wear underpants.

I didn't wear underpants with my trapeze costume. I couldn't. It rode too high on my hips, and the thick white tights would show a line. I changed inside the bus, which was still parked next to the fairgrounds. It had been on the road only a few days and already was beginning to smell like sour milk. No one was allowed to use the Greyhound-style toilet on board, and the door to the refrigerator was broken, so that every time it went around a sharp curve, the door burst open and sent milk (it was always milk, I don't know why) flying onto the ugly orange carpet.

At 7:15, before an eight o'clock show, it seemed as if everyone on Chautauqua was on the bus at the same time, doing last-minute makeup or trying to find the right band jacket to wear. The standard costume for parades and shows was a marching-band-style jacket and black "stupid pants" (wraparound cotton). I stripped in the back of the bus, which had taken on the asexuality of a dressing room. Buttocks, thighs, and breasts were unnoticed in the rush to get organized before the show. Everyone focused inward in that half hour before showtime, cheerful mostly, but distracted. Checking props, costumes, hair, and lipstick, as if about to depart on an overnight journey. Angela and The Girls Who Wear Glasses were passing a brandy bottle back and forth. Ivan Karamazov was standing outside impatiently; he had been trying to get the band to form up for ten minutes already, and his eight-year-old son, Jason, who played trombone like his father, needed help tying up a pair of stupid pants that were way too long. Finally Ivan blew his band leader's whistle three times, and the band formed up.

They marched onstage and played the opening number, "Picnic Time for Teddy Bears," the traditional Chautauqua and Country Fair opening of the show. Since I didn't play an instrument, I cartwheeled next to the band, toward the back. All of the free-form members of the parade stayed at the back—the kids dressed up in makeshift fairy costumes. Artis blew bubbles and sometimes allowed a small human to perch on his shoulders. Anyone else who wanted to join in grabbed a percussion instrument out of a big green trunk. As soon as they heard the band, the audience started to applaud, and a wave of relief rippled through me. There were no more rehearsals, no second chances, and they were on our side. It was opening night.

I was too nervous to watch much of the first act. Always ready too soon, I laid out my straw mat behind the stage trailer and kept stretching. It seemed that each individual act lengthened with the laughs, as the performers found their timing with a good audience. Intermission was kept short because, though the show was going well, it was moving slowly, and Dmitri wanted the break to be under ten minutes. Magical Mystical Michael was to open the second act with a quick magic trick and then do my introduction. The band resumed with a couple of opening numbers, and Dmitri left the clarinet section early to see if I was ready. I was as ready as I could be, and he gave Michael the go. As soon as Michael walked onstage, I had about one minute. I took off the sweatshirt and wool tights that I had been wearing to keep warmed up and put chalk on my hands. It was just getting dark, and I knew that I would feel the spotlight as soon as I got out there. I just hoped that it wouldn't blind me. Dmitri was next to me, ready for me to climb onto his shoulders and make my entrance.

"Take your time," he said. "You'll be great. They've never seen anything like this, so don't worry about impressing them."

"Okay." I tried to smile at him.

"Take your time."

"Right. I'll be fine."

Michael came to the end of his routine. Dmitri smiled at me and touched me lightly at the small of my back. I breathed again, tried to tell myself to keep breathing. Putting one hand in each of his, I climbed up his back to his shoulders. Michael was introducing me now. I didn't have any idea what he was going to say, and I just caught scraps of it.

". . . direct from New York . . . ladies and gentlemen! Francesca Devianté!"

I was on. Stepping out from behind the trailer, Dmitri walked steadily up to the bar, and I held out my arms in a balletic pose, smiling, always smiling. I could hardly see anything at first, I was so scared, and I looked for the bar. Once we got underneath it, Dmitri pulled down firmly on the back of my knees as he rose onto demi-pointe so that I could reach the trapeze. I grabbed the bar, and the music started up. Dmitri let go, I swung my legs back and up over the bar, and I was there, letting go of the bar with my hands for the first balance and allowing myself actually to see the audience for the first time. The crowd looked huge to me. I held out my arms in an image of rigid effortlessness. Breathe. Smile.

I wasn't expecting the applause. God knows why, since they had been such a good audience for the first half. But I was surprised by the response. It was nothing I had thought about or planned for, and I rushed through the routine, not giving them enough of a chance to applaud. I was listening more to the music than the crowd. The applause sounded far away, and when I allowed myself to look at them, smiling, blowing kisses, they looked far away. My concentration was absolute, too absolute really, and I didn't let them into my awareness. It was all over very quickly. I don't even know how I got into my last move, but suddenly there I was, hanging from one arm and blowing kisses. Dmitri guided my feet to his shoulders from below, and I found my balance and let go of the bar. Dipping forward, I jumped from his shoulders to the stage in a move we had practiced. The band kept playing through my applause, unsure of where to stop. I kept bowing, expecting the band to finish up, but it was a guessing game for all of us at that point. The band was waiting for me, as I waited for the band, and the audience applauded somewhere off in the distance. As soon as I felt it was graceful to do so, I left the stage, unable to catch Ivan's eye to tell the band to stop. It was surreal. Dmitri started kissing me as soon as I got offstage. He pulled me in and tossed me into the air. We were giggling and talking at once, forgetting the necessary quiet of backstage. We both remembered where we were at the same time, and I whispered, repeating the same question over and over again, "How was it?"

"They loved it. Couldn't you tell?"

"I don't know. Yes. I mean, I'm not sure. At least I got through it without falling!"

I could hardly catch my breath, but I couldn't stop smiling.

"Come on," Dmitri whispered. "You've got to help Michael and me. We're on next."

I followed him into the trailer. Sandy Bradley was on-stage doing her musical number set in a cafe. She was a blonde with a cloud of curls and a wry smile. She looked perfect for the role of a down-and-out babe in a diner. Inside the trailer, Magical Mystical Michael was halfway into the two-man straitjacket. He waved a straitjacketed sleeve at me.

"Good job, kiddo." He turned to Dmitri. "You got the silverware?"

"Yeah. Here, Francesca, hand this to Michael, will you? One piece at a time."

Dmitri stripped down to an undershirt while I handed Michael pieces of silverware which he hid somewhere inside the leather contraption. It was covered with straps and buckles.

"Okay, get in," ordered Michael, and Dmitri slipped his head under Michael's arm and into the straitjacket. They had their arms wrapped around each other and strapped across the back, so that they looked like some strange two-headed armless torso.

"Now do up the rest of the straps," Michael whispered, and I started buckling and tightening, under the crotch, over the shoulders, across the neck, and down the back. I kept waiting for him to tell me to leave a certain strap undone, to let me in on the trick, but he never said anything except "Hurry up," so I buckled them in tight and couldn't see how they were going to pull this off.

"It's been a while since we've done this," Dmitri whispered to Michael.

"Yeah. Maybe we should've rehearsed." Michael grinned.

They took a beat, looking at each other, then, simultaneously: "Nah . . ." And they were on.

The band played a waltz as they struggled and camped it up onstage. I watched from behind the band. They rolled around on the ground for a while, and eventually, inevitably, the silverware came tumbling out. Somehow they got their arms out from behind their backs and over their heads, and from there they worked their way out of the jacket. Both rumpled, shirts pulled half up, they took a triumphant bow, hair wild with static electricity.

Artis came out next, and he changed the atmosphere in an instant. It was finally getting dark, and the lights made the stage glow with pinks and yellows. He looked like a patchwork court jester—with an attitude. The first thing he did was to attack the audience for the overall somnambulism of the American public, exhorting them to use their right to vote, and then he apologized and sang a love song. Artis sang unaccompanied by any instruments and stood quite still as he delivered the words, unlike his spoon playing, which sent his entire body into a leaping whirl of rhythm. Artis had written songs about practically everything, from his notorious number about circumcision ("I want my foreskin back," went the refrain) to the economy ("Do you own it? Or do you owe on it?"). He dealt in equal measures of anger and love, and tonight he sang only love songs. After the songs he brought out his spoons and went to a squat. He started quietly, with a spoon against a tuning fork that rang out for a long time over the field.

Though it was an outdoor show, the audience was quiet, and Artis took his time. First he moved to flat wooden sticks, then wooden spoons, and finally silver spoons. He dropped and picked up new instruments in a split second, and everything fit with the rhythm in his head once he had established the groove. I had seen Artis perform for years, but it had usually been on the street or at the Fair, where there was a lot of ambient noise. Tonight, everyone was listening, and Artis went wild, blending tones and leaping from one place to another onstage as he crouched and hopped and swung his arm in a pinwheel against his body—hitting the spoons against his thighs.

After Artis came The Girls Who Wear Glasses, Rebo and Jan. They both carried guitars and wore fifties-style glasses and black skirts. They sounded great together— Jan had a gutsy blues voice, while Rebo sailed above her with clear harmonies. They sang mostly original material, songs with a sense of humor and a love song thrown in every now and then. Rebo had a sexy way of swinging her hips from side to side as she sang, and they both had a tendency to crack each other up onstage and bring the audience in on their private jokes. I had heard their songs many, many times, but I wasn't tired of them yet, and I closed my eyes and leaned against the back of the trailer, staring up at the circle of night sky that was slowly moving down to the edges of the horizon.

I went out front to watch the Karamazovs. They did their juggling improvisation number called "Jazz," which is a long juggling session in which they throw unplanned, impossible throws to each other, and when they miss (which happens all the time, but the Karamazovs have trained their audiences to look beyond a club dropped on the ground), they retrieve the club from wherever it lands, even when it has landed in the audience, behind the stage set, or in the bushes. They have been doing this number for years, but since it is an improvisation it is a little different every night, and the audience always loves it.

Their final number was the real showstopper, however. All evening Ivan and Dmitri Karamazov had been the emcees of the show, tying it together with introductions and jokes. At the same time they had been introducing nine "objects of terror"—a cleaver, a raw egg, a bottle of champagne, and a chunk of dry ice, among other things. Throughout the show these objects had been slowly accumulating on a small easel onstage, and now the Brothers came out to perform the "Terror" trick. They juggled all nine objects together, which was amazing in itself, but as the grand finale they finished with the raw egg sizzling in a saucepan over a flaming torch and champagne in glasses for each of them to toast the audience and then toss champagne all over the front row. It was a wonderful bit, and the audience loved it.

There was a standing ovation, and Ivan led the band into the last number, which began with Cici Dawn, The Girls Who Wear Glasses, and me singing and dancing a rap number Jan had written for the finale. The whole cast and band quickly joined us onstage for a free-for-all dance number, and we jumped off the stage down to the audience to get them up and dancing with us. This became my favorite part of the show as the summer went on. The band was hot, and whether or not the audience could be cajoled into dancing with us, we all let loose and had a great time goofing off with one another at the end. As the band came to a stop and everyone threw their hands up as if it were a Broadway musical, Dmitri took the microphone and yelled to the audience: "Now go out there and save the world!"

That night there was a birthday party in the dormitories for Susan. Still possessed by the show, I wasn't in the mood for a party, though I put in an appearance. People sat on the edge of orange couches and ate pretzels. Once again I was reminded of boarding school. I was silently processing everything that had happened that night. My act kept going through my head in slow motion—where I could have waited longer, how I could have made the drops seem more dramatic. It takes so much preparation for a few minutes in the light, I always want it to be perfect. I slipped out the door when no one was looking. I didn't want to explain anything to Angela or Dmitri tonight. I needed to sort out the pictures in my head. All of those faces looking up at me from upside down. Later, when Dmitri came to my room, I sent him away. I didn't know how to make him understand that I wanted to have every part of me to myself tonight. All of my stretched, aching, joyful body, which had nothing left to give.

CHAPTER 5

IVAN STOOD AT the back of the dormitories and blew three short blasts followed by a long wail on the shofar. The curved ram's horn, which is used in synagogues on the Jewish high holidays of Rosh Hashanah and Yom Kippur, was also used, traditionally, to call the tribe together, and Ivan had been using his to do just this. His son, Jason, had a shofar, too, and always looked up, thrilled, when he got a squawk out of the little horn. College students walking by in their white shorts looked around, startled to see the disparate group gathered in their backyard. We were forming a Circle, and the shofar sounded strange, discordant notes that made me imagine a donkey braying from some Jerusalem hillside.

This morning the Circle was more logistical than spiritual. Everyone seemed to be feeling pretty good about the show and the workshops. They would get better, of course, but we had gotten through our first day, and no one in the audience had found out how haphazard it felt to us before the show. We had a long drive ahead; over to Salmon, Idaho, in the northern part of the state. Salmon was so small that the local kids called the Chautauqua "the movies" because that was the only other form of entertainment, except television, that they had ever seen.

I rode in The Scenicruiser; Dmitri was driving. I had never ridden on the bus before, though I had visited the Karamazovs in various cities around the country over the years and had sometimes gone to sit on the bus in the parking lot of the theatre for a glass of wine after the show. During Chautauqua, the bus was filled with people, especially the younger generation. It had an upper and a lower deck, both with small tables where people could sit and play cards or read. The upholstery and the orange shag carpet on the walls and ceiling were hideous, and the whole bus smelled funky, but there were windows on all sides and a good sound system.

Two new people joined us in Boise: Pat Warner and Dennis Perrin. Both doctors and both original members of the Chautauqua, they were going to be with us for about a week. At its inception, the Chautauqua had been envisioned as a group of healers, educators, and entertainers joining forces, and the workshops were an outgrowth of that idea. Somehow this had led the very first Chautauqua to include both a coven of witches and a splinter group of

"The Love Family," a strange, pseudo-Christian sect based in the Northwest. I had heard rumors that the "unicorn" (a goat whose horns were bound together at birth, which was later sold to the Ringling Bros. and Barnum & Bailey Circus, causing a scandal among the animal rights groups) was also on that journey with its breeders. Pat and Dennis had been around in those days and were still involved, and though neither of them could take the time away from the rest of their work to go on the whole Chautauqua, they were dropping in.

Pat is a big man, over six feet tall, with a walrus mustache and a long blond ponytail. He is one of the founders of the Gesundheit Institute, an association of medical professionals in Virginia who believe in the healing power of laughter. All of the Gesundheit doctors also work as clowns—real clowns, with red noses and such; at least, that's what Pat wore everywhere he went. He travels all over the world trying to raise money to build a hospital that will offer the kind of care these doctors think people really need when they are sick. This includes keeping people laughing as well as treating their physical ills. The doctors also want to be able to offer this kind of care for free. The hospital sounded like an impossible dream to me, but a good one. Still, something about Pat makes you believe it might happen. He seems to shine, with his big hands and a smile that is at once silly and sad, like all good clowns'.

Dennis is curly-haired and young-looking, with an East Coast energy that I connected with right away. We talked politics on the bus that day, and it was like a good cold wind. I hadn't had a decent political discussion since I had left New York a month ago, and I missed it. The massacre in Tiananmen Square was still recent history, but nobody on the Chautauqua talked about it. So Dennis and I jabbered politics while Dmitri drove the bus.

Dennis had bought a box of poker chips and a deck of cards in Boise, and pretty soon a group of us gathered in the back of the bus to play five-card stud and blackjack. We laughed for hours. There was a sliding door between the "blue room" at the back of the bus, where we were playing, and the rest of the upper deck. Every now and then someone would poke his head in and then pull back quickly when he was greeted by a shower of plastic poker chips. By the end, Dennis had pretty much cleaned the rest of us out. There was one huge kitty left in the middle when suddenly, as if by common consent, we all dove for it and threw the chips into the air. They flooded everything, nooks and crannies of the bedding, people's hair. The game was over.

I lay in the blue room for the rest of the trip, talking with Dennis and later, when Fyodor took over the driving, Dmitri. We were really in the mountains now. There was less vegetation, and the hillsides were rocky and brown. I could tell from the way Dmitri and Dennis talked about Salmon, Idaho, that it was one of their favorite places. We would be camping by a river where there were natural hot springs nearby. I liked just lying there, quietly, listening to these two talk; they had known each other for so long.

Sometime in the midafternoon we stopped at a truck stop to fuel the bus. None of the other vehicles had been in sight for hours, but the bus traveled faster than most, and both The Rubber Chicken and the truck that pulled the stage trailer were on their last legs. Sandy Bradley's van, The Mother Hen, was keeping an eye on that end of the caravan, and there was no point in waiting, so we pressed on. Dmitri and I made sandwiches for everybody, passing them out the window to a trestle table that somebody had set up in a hurry. Miraculously, vanilla ice cream and root beer appeared, and we all had root beer floats in the parking lot.

We didn't arrive until dusk, with still no sign of the other vehicles. I was starting to worry about Angela in Psycho Car. I hoped it hadn't broken down, though I knew she had Max and Rebo with her, so she wouldn't be alone. I had tried not to feel guilty about going in the bus, but I kept thinking about her. Dmitri parked on the far side of a wide river that looked black and fast-moving in the twilight. The bridge wouldn't support the weight of the bus, so we walked over it, carrying our packs and tents. Not having The Rubber Chicken meant no supper; there weren't many supplies on The Scenicruiser. Parents made do with peanut butter sandwiches for the kids, and the rest of us did without.

Our host for the next three days was Dugout Dick, an old mountain man who lived on the shores of the river in caves he dug into the hillside. He used the doors and windows of abandoned cars to make the front walls of these little dwellings, and the glass glinted out of the dirt unexpectedly. The door of a VW bug was stuck into the side of the mountain in a slash of rusted metal. Dick came out to meet us. He had been letting the Chautauqua camp there all the years they had been coming to Salmon. He said very little. He was really a kind of hermit, I thought. That night was the closest I got to having a conversation with him. He stayed at one of the caves high above the river while we were there and played his harmonica in the evenings.

It was a clear night, and the full moon hadn't yet reached over the mountains into our little valley. Everyone was tired and hungry but happy to be off the bus at last. Dmitri was clearly excited. After exchanging a few words with Dugout Dick, he took my hand and walked with me past the general camping area to find a place to pitch our tent.

"Wait 'til tomorrow. We can go see the ice caves."

"Ice caves?"

"Dugout Dick's version of a refrigerator."

"Does he live here all year alone?"

"He rents out the caves, sometimes. To artists, or writers. People who are poor but need to get away and work."

"What about supplies? Is there a town nearby?"

"There's a gas station/tavern pretty close. We'll do a show there Saturday night. But the closest town is Salmon, twenty miles away."

"And the winters?"

"It gets really cold up here, but he stays. I guess he just hides in his caves like a bear."

"What about a wife, or a girlfriend . . . anybody?"

"Sometimes the River Goddess stays here—but she's not his girlfriend."

"The River Goddess? Oh, come on, give me a break. Who is the River Goddess?"

"She's this woman who lives here sometimes. Down by the river."

"Well, what do you mean, River Goddess?"

"It's just that . . . well, it makes sense when you see how she is."

Suddenly I thought I had figured something out. "So— you and the River Goddess?"

"No! I mean, not really . . ." He was blushing. Even under his dark skin, in the twilight, I could tell.

I laughed, knowing I had him. "Not *really*? What does that mean?"

"We shared a sleeping bag one night, but nothing happened."

"Oh, God! How many times have I heard that? 'We were in the same bed, but we still had our underwear on, and—' "

We were both laughing, even though he kept denying it.

"Does she *call* herself a goddess?"

"Well, yes, kind of."

"You mean she's just *kind* of a goddess?"

"No, no! Just forget it, okay?"

"Is she here now? I mean, she'll probably put some kind of spell on me and turn me into a slug."

"She wouldn't do that. I don't think that she's here now anyway."

"Lucky me . . ."

After setting up the tent, we built a bonfire on the little

pebble beach next to the river. It was a small group—still no sign of Psycho Car, but Faith and Allen had made it. They hadn't seen anyone else on the road. Allen brought out some chips and salsa that he had in his van, and we devoured them. They were good for a moment, but then they reminded us of how hungry we were. Faith broke out her guitar to stop us from thinking about food, and we sang moon songs. We were still waiting for the moon to break out over the ridge across the river. We sang "Blue Moon," "Paper Moon," "Moon River," and on and on. I sat back, leaning against Dmitri's knees. I felt safe. It's just my longing for comfort, I thought.

The moon slipped up over the ridge, clean as new chalk, just as I had forgotten about looking for it. Everyone cheered, as if we had brought it up ourselves by serenading it. Maybe we had. It felt just barely possible in that place. I can't remember who started it, but Dmitri, Faith, and a few of the other seasoned Chautauquans started making noises about the "Moon Ceremony." They made us all get up and turn our backs to the moon. I prepared myself for another hippie spiritual ritual and waited to see what would come next. I hoped we weren't going to chant or anything. I'd rather sing cowboy songs. Dmitri suddenly gave the order: "Pants down!"

We all bent over, giggling, pulled down our pants, and mooned the moon.

. . .

We woke up to find that everyone had arrived during the night. The Rubber Chicken was there, complete with our official cook, Alex, who was making an incredible breakfast of waffles, raspberries, and yogurt. The idea of serving that many people out of the door of a school bus was overwhelming to me. Alex was a miracle worker. She kept feeding us delicious meals, one after another, in parking lots and at ferry landings. I also saw Psycho Car parked down the road, so I knew that Angela had made it. I wondered what her story would be. I knew there would be a story; there always was with Psycho Car.

Besides the Chautauquans, we saw a family of white Rastafarians hanging around the cook bus. They must have been renting a cave from Dugout Dick. It was impossible to tell how old the father and mother were; their hair was white and woven into thick clumps all over their heads. The man's body looked hard and muscled, while the woman looked tired, though she could have simply been stoned. There were three or four small children with white-blond hair running around, who were obviously theirs. The children wore no shirts or shoes, had long hair and feet as tough as little hooves. It was impossible to tell which were girls and which were boys. The parents kept their distance from our group, but the children immediately lined up when food was served and later played down at the river with the Chautauqua kids. They played very differently, however. They were truly feral children, utterly fearless, their faces stained with dirt and the fine dust of dried river mud and sagebrush, their eyes older than their bodies. There was a kind of purity to their filth, they had such an animal quality. I wondered how long they had been here, and how often they saw other children.

We had two days off before we did the show in Salmon. Dmitri wanted to head up to the hot springs right after breakfast, bringing our sleeping bags so that we could stay overnight. I had been to only one natural hot spring before, when Gwen and I hitchhiked west through British Columbia ten years before. It had been basically a mud hole near a river down a logging road, and though it was nice and warm, I wouldn't have wanted to spend the night there. It wasn't hard to see how Dmitri felt about this place, though, and I wanted to get up into the mountains after driving through them for so long.

Alex let us forage in The Rubber Chicken for supplies, and we filled Dmitri's pack with fruit, cheese, and bread. We also filled a plastic jug with water. It was going to be a long walk into "town" (the gas station) if we couldn't hitch a ride, and then there was the trail up to the hot springs. Dmitri wanted to try to call Anita, the woman who was waiting for him at home, from the gas station. I didn't know whether to call her his girlfriend or not, and he wasn't even sure if she was going back to his home or not. He had been trying to call, but she was never there. I was trying to stay out of it. I wanted more than anything just to stay in the present moment with him. I can buy into thinking about the future with a man so easily that it scares me.

We walked across the bridge and over to the road along the river. The mountain went straight up on one side, the road a pencil scratch on the side of it, a two-lane highway. A few cars went by, looking at us suspiciously without stopping. Dmitri could have been taken for a Native

American, with his dark skin and long black braid. We walked by a farm whose fields were bright green with midsummer corn. It looked unnatural in this scrub landscape where even the river was brown. Two Irish wolfhounds loped toward us, barking and running along their side of the river to be sure that we knew that this was their kingdom. There was a shout from the farmhouse, and a woman came out wearing a dress and high rubber boots.

"You with the Chautauqua?" she yelled across to us.

We called back that we were, not knowing if it would be in our favor or not.

"Need a ride to town?"

She walked around to the front of the house, and pretty soon a white pickup, with both dogs in the back, was headed our way. She had recognized Dmitri from last year's show, and she wanted to know if we were going to perform at the local tavern, which had been the tradition when the group camped at Dugout's place. When Dmitri told her yes, tomorrow night, she said that she wouldn't miss it. After she dropped us off, Dmitri explained that this was the "Bob" show, so named because it was organized by Bob, the clarinet player. It was a show that Chautauqua had started doing for themselves as a joke. No admission was charged, no publicity sent out; it had somehow become a tradition. The only rule was that if you were a performer you had to do whatever you didn't usually do in the show. The Karamazov Brothers didn't juggle, Magical Mystical Michael didn't do magic. Rehearsal was out of the question. Musicians would juggle, and a mime artist would deliver a monologue. I wondered what I would do but kept quiet about it for the moment.

Dmitri went over to the public phone booth, and I went into the store to buy postcards. It was the kind of place that sold pictures of enormous fish superimposed on a lake scene, with a jokey remark written below. I love that kind of postcard, so I bought several and some licorice whips. It looked as if Dmitri had reached somebody on the phone. I started to stuff myself with the licorice. The day was already hot, and the air conditioner dripped into a metal pan at the far corner of the store. I looked over the menu—French dip sandwiches, milkshakes, and tuna melts. The man behind the counter didn't pay any attention to me. He looked to be in his sixties and was staring grimly at the coffee machine as it peed a steady stream of fresh coffee into the glass pot below it. Dmitri came back inside.

"She wasn't home. I left another message on the machine."

What kind of message could you leave, I wondered. I leaned into him, tense, relieved, not knowing what to say. I wanted her to be home. I wanted to be on the other side of this, no matter where that ended up being.

"I'll keep trying," he said.

I kissed him. "How about fries and a shake?"

He smiled, not very wide, and held me tight while he looked at the menu. The air conditioner went ping . . . ping . . . into the metal pan.

"Okay," he said. "Last chance for fried food before the hot springs."

We sat at one of the three tables in the tiny dining room. The man behind the counter took his time coming over to get our order, although we were the only ones in the place. I ordered a black-and-white, which is what we call a shake with vanilla ice cream and chocolate syrup back east. I had to explain it to the man, and he sighed heavily; he had known we were going to be trouble. Sitting there at the table together, I had the familiar feeling that Dmitri and I had been together forever, that we'd sat in a million cafes like this all over America. I played nervously with the salt shaker and didn't know what to say about his phone call.

The fries and shake were fantastic. It had been a long time since I had been in a restaurant at all, and the grease and salt and sugar were just what we both wanted. The trail up to the hot springs started about a quarter of a mile from the cafe. I automatically converted this distance into five city blocks, a unit of measurement I could grasp more easily.

"How far is it from there up to the hot springs?"

"A couple of miles."

Forty blocks. It was about noon and getting into the hottest part of the day. We paid up, got out onto the road, and started up the trail. There was a stream that ran down the mountain, and the path went beside it, a thin, brilliant stripe of green all the way up. Everywhere else was dry and brittle. Big sagebrushes grew on all sides. I loved their smell—a dry, clean scent. Dmitri walked ahead of me, keeping an eye out for rattlesnakes, which he said were likely to be sunning themselves on the trail. That information heightened my awareness quite a bit, but as we kept climbing I got too tired to think about it. I was in better shape than I had ever been in my life, from doing trapeze and training all spring, but I had to stop and rest at least three times on the way up. It was steep but beautiful. We didn't talk a lot except to show each other a rock or sagebrush that was especially big. Dmitri cut some sage with his knife and put it together in a bundle to make a "smudge," the Native American cleansing ritual that we had done at the first Circle. I held it up to my face and rubbed some leaves between my fingers. I wanted my whole body to smell like that forever.

Steam from the hot springs curled up into the clear blue skies, disappearing faster than smoke. There was a series of pools going down the mountain, set close together, maybe six pools in all. Waterfalls ran between each level, some hot and some cold. A few of the pools looked as if they had been blocked off on purpose with large stones, while others had been formed by the water simply wearing away at the rock. It felt like an ancient place. The water is warm because it passes close to levels of hot earth deep inside the planet. The pools that are fed by just the hot streams of water are almost unbearable. The pools here were clear and not too deep, and you could sit comfortably up to your neck and shoulders.

No one else was there, and the silence was enormous. We stripped and stepped into one of the pools. I gasped at the heat and knew I had to take my time. Dmitri went

right in until he floated, half-sitting in the spring. We were
in the crevice of the mountains, and from here I could see
how high up we were. A red-tailed hawk circled slowly
above us in the heat.

Dmitri lay his head back on a rock and let his body
relax. I made my way in and floated next to him so that
the field of electricity around our bodies merged, but we
hardly touched. We talked. We talked for hours while our
bodies turned soft and molten in the water. I wore a big
white cotton sun hat, and we dipped it under a cold wa-
terfall to pour water over our faces. The heat of the day
took away our appetites, but we drank from the water jug.
We talked about having reached an age where none of our
choices seemed as clear as they had even five years ago.
It felt as if the water were sloughing off our earlier lives
with our layers of dead skin. There was no room for pretense
anymore. I couldn't keep telling him I was holding back
from him; it was too late. I wept for my nakedness in front
of him, and he made promises to me that he never should
have, touching my skin as if it were paper. We both knew
that it was too late to go slow—though that wasn't what we
said out loud. Our hearts were passed back and forth, palm
to palm, in the sulfurous water.

The others began to arrive, in twos and threes, then
finally in a large, noisy group. We had no idea how much
time had passed and were suddenly starving. We raised
ourselves out of the pool and made our sandwiches as the
others dipped in and let out their breaths in long sighs,
just as we had. It was a shock to be around everybody else
after having been alone for so long. The group felt different

up here; people were on their own today, no longer defined by their role on the Chautauqua, and nothing was required.

By the time it began to get dark there were twenty people in a pool, rolling like a litter of puppies in the water. Candles were stuck on the rocks while we watched the white streak of light from the moon grow wider on the opposite mountainside. Pat stood up at the edge of the pool, looking like a medieval giant with his long hair and huge arms, and began to recite *The Love Song of J. Alfred Prufrock*, his voice echoing around the rock walls of the pool and up over the ridge. After Prufrock came Dylan Thomas, then someone remembered a scrap of Shakespeare.

Much, much later Dmitri and I crept away while the rest of them were still going at it. We went to a rock ledge that was wide and dry and hung out over the valley like a shelf. Gathering up some tall grasses, we made a bed and put our sleeping bags on top of it. I slept deeply, without dreaming, every bone turned to liquid under my skin. At sunrise we both woke up and saw the light pour back into the valley, then fell asleep again. Some hours later we got up, washed at the pools, and came back to our ledge for a breakfast of chocolate, grapes, and cheese. Benjamin, the resident composer, crept over the rocks to join us. He was one of the few who had spent the night; almost everyone else had gone back down the trail by moonlight. We shared our breakfast, and Dmitri read aloud from Neruda's love poems, which I had brought along, in his Catalonian-accented Spanish.

Before we left, Dmitri and I each cut off a lock of hair,

wrapped it in a bundle with some sage, and left it under a rock near where we slept, working magic on ourselves. Halfway down the trail we found Faith Petric walking steadily down with her little pack and a walking stick. She had hiked all the way up and spent the night up at the springs in a hammock. She smiled and teased Dmitri when he told her that, at seventy-four, she was an inspiration to us.

"Don't need to sleep as much as you people do," she said. "There's too much to see."

. . .

That night was the Bob show. Bob was a small, dark-haired man who spoke with a Brooklyn nasality that I liked. He and his wife, Mary, had a baby along on this Chautauqua; their first, Gregory. He had a small tuft of red hair, which shot up from the middle of his head, and a pair of tiny eyebrows which were always questioning. His little round eyes and quizzical look made him the spitting image of Tintin, the French comic-book character. Bob was a quiet guy, an unlikely candidate for the master of ceremonies, which is exactly what made him perfect for the Bob show.

Angela and I put together a rock band in about fifteen minutes, out behind the bar. We wore black mini-skirts, called ourselves "Live Bait" (after the signs at all the little rural stores), and sang some Springsteen songs. What we lacked in rehearsal time, we made up for in attitude. This was the night that "Junior Chautauquavitz," the kids' rap group, was born. Four of them, ranging from twelve to seven years old, delivered a rap they had written themselves (with a little help). The message was good—save the planet and all that—but the best part was watching the kids act cool and tough.

Junior Chautauquavitz ended up being a permanent part of the show. The highlight, however, was Benjamin and Dmitri's folk duo, "Rabbis without a Cause." They wore Jewish prayer shawls over their shoulders, Benjamin strummed the guitar, and they did a takeoff on a Bob Dylan song, "I'll Be Your Rabbi Tonight," followed by "Ghost Rabbis in the Sky." I don't know if the Jewish humor went right over the audience's heads in Idaho, but we all thought it was hysterical, and the locals seemed to have a good time. Everyone on Chautauqua ended up singing those songs for the rest of the tour. Two years later, a couple of young comedians from Miami came out with a Jewish rap song which rocketed up the charts. Dmitri and Benjamin had missed another get-rich-quick scheme by leaving the "Rabbis" in that country tavern.

Everyone stayed late at the bar—the place was packed. Angela and I bought beers for our band and took snapshots of what would probably be our first and last appearance. We got back to camp late, and there wasn't any campfire. We were going to have to break camp early and do a show in Salmon tomorrow afternoon. Salmon was in the heart of the "Aryan Nation": neo-Nazis and white supremacists had settled into this part of America after the Vietnam War. They found it appealing because of the abundance of wilderness and lack of ethnicity in the general population. Dmitri had said that they came out for the Chautauqua shows, but how could anybody know who had an arsenal at home. We did know that they were headquartered some-

where up in these mountains, and they weren't waiting for
the end of the world, they were working toward it. I thought
about Dmitri and Benjamin singing in the bar in their
prayer shawls as we watched the dappled moon crest over
the ridge.

CHAPTER 6

GOING DOWN A mountain pass into Montana, The Rubber Chicken lost its brakes. The Chicken had left early that morning after our show in Salmon, Idaho, while it was still dark out. The cook-bus crew was hoping to get a jump on the 350-mile journey to Browning, Montana, and set up the kitchen for the rest of us. The Mother Hen, which was traveling in caravan with the Chicken to keep an eye on its progress, had its CB on, and the passengers heard Max's voice as the accident was happening. Like the eerie tapes from plane crashes, they later told the story to the rest of us over and over again. The bus was picking up speed, and Max kept slamming on the brakes, but there was simply nothing there. What

105

no one had told him before he started driving the vehicle was that the more you pump air brakes, the less they work, so in fact he was systematically bleeding the brakes. Yelling into the radio for the van to stay back, Max steered the bus into the side of the mountain, scraping off the door and throwing foodstuffs and pots and pans everywhere. Alex was on board with her five-year-old daughter, but no one was hurt. The mountain finally stopped the bus; its side smashed into the dirt. The Mother Hen brought everyone back to the camp in Salmon, and in the end The Rubber Chicken had to be towed into Missoula, Montana, a college town that wasn't too far from the Blackfoot reservation where the rest of us were heading.

The show in Salmon had almost been rained out. Storms passed through all day, and I kept my trapeze off the rigging until the very last moment. Great black thunderheads raced in out of nowhere, dropped their load of rain, and moved on just as quickly, leaving the sky blue and wet. In the late afternoon, everyone stopped working as a double rainbow arched over the stage. A small river ran next to the park we were performing and camping in, and just below the surface of the field lay a rocky streambed, a relic of the days when the river had filled the basin of land that had been turned into a smooth green lawn by the city of Salmon. I hacked at the ground all afternoon with the pickax. It was so hard that some of the stage crew took pity on me and offered to help. We took turns with the sledge hammer and pickax, and by the time we dug the holes deep enough to put up the rigging I was streaked in mud and dust. While Allen tied down the last of the ropes,

I climbed up over the bank of the river and started to strip. I was down to my underpants when some teenagers came floating down the river in inner tubes. I grabbed my shirt and squatted down, silent, as they floated by shouting at each other, oblivious to the potential surprise that would have made such a good story for them that summer. After three days at Dugout Dick's, I had forgotten that we were back among the civilized in Salmon, Idaho, where people wore bathing suits when they swam in state parks.

There were a few tires and small wooden floats tied to the bridge over the river that acted as surfboards for the local boys, who stayed on them all day, their taut white bodies plastered against the spinning water. The bridge was made of railroad trestles, and you could see the water rushing below through the gaps. Fyodor Karamazov had been driving the bus when we arrived that morning, and he made everyone get off before crossing the bridge, never explaining why. Then he revved up the motor until diesel fumes poured out of the back, and while the Chautauquans and the local boys watched, he gunned the bus as fast as possible across the bridge, afraid it might collapse under the weight. The Scenicruiser, at forty feet, was almost as long as the bridge, so it was over quickly. But it was terrifying to watch the huge machine lumber over the tiny bridge as Fyodor gripped the wheel, hands and face gone white for the brief second I saw him as he flashed past us.

The parade in Salmon was a big success despite the weather. Local kids had decorated their bikes in the plastic Day-Glo that has found its way to every corner of America, and they formed two phalanxes of color on either side of our marching band. The show was performed in a heavy, gray humidity that night, but the rain held off, and families came with children, picnics, and rain gear.

The rain hit during the finale, and the band scrambled onstage from the bandstand in a rush to keep their instruments dry. The audience hoisted umbrellas and stayed until the end, a small pack of black pointed domes over neon rain ponchos. As soon as the last note of the finale was sung, everyone dropped character and any awareness of the audience in the rush to protect their props, instruments, and costumes. I ran for a ladder to take down my trapeze before the velvet-covered ropes got wet. The concession people were boxing up the T-shirts, albums, and tapes that we sold, while all of the musicians ran for their cases. Susan, who was also in charge of costumes, yelled at people to run for the bus and strip before their band jackets and stupid pants got soaked. The trapeze rig came down in record time. Allen wanted to leave it up overnight rather than take it down in the rain, but Dmitri said it had to come down and get loaded up that night, since we were leaving for Montana first thing in the morning. It would be all we could do to break camp, eat breakfast, and go.

The stage crew, which was primarily made up of band members, was taking down the lights while Abe, a wiry New Yorker in his early fifties, cursed and yelled at everyone from his ladder. He was the technical director, and he was in his element as the rain poured down and people scurried below him. By the time the stage, yurts, tipi, and trapeze rig were down, the rain had lightened to a steady drizzle, but only a few people had tents that were well enough made to withstand a real downpour.

There was a small shelter behind the stage, a metal pavilion with rest rooms and a concession area. People pulled their sleeping bags out of their tents and slept there, or grabbed bunks in The Scenicruiser. Angela, who was in a vile mood because her saxophone case had gotten wet on the inside, stormed past me with her sleeping bag and muttered that she was going to sleep in Psycho Car.

I hadn't unpacked my tent since Boise. Angela had been right about my move into Dmitri's tent. My tent (Psycho Tent, we had named it, long before Psycho Car came along) actually belonged to my friend Fon DuCaniveaux, who was one of the West Coast members of the Royale Famille DuCaniveaux, the troupe we had started on the streets of Paris, and she performed with the troupe every summer at the Country Fair. We were tent mates during the second DuCaniveaux tour of Europe (our version of a tour was to live in vans, camp out, and play the streets and the bars for hat money), and she had been at the Country Fair with Psycho Tent many times. We always decorated it with plastic toys or a pink flamingo outside the door, and we regularly lost items into the "black hole" inside the tent. This was the only way we could explain how important possessions always disappeared at the Country Fair. Occasionally, a year or two later, Psycho Tent would spit up something that hadn't agreed with it: a lost watch, a favorite T-shirt, a camping pass from the Fair.

It was the best tent in the world for looks and personality

with its faded blue cover and bits of aluminum stars trailing off the rain fly, but it was a fair-weather tent. Once, in Europe, we had covered it in a huge sheet of clear plastic to protect ourselves from the rain, and we barely survived the night, suffocated as we were by the trapped air. We never tried to fence in Psycho Tent again. Now Dmitri, who loved to camp, claimed that his tent was good enough to keep us dry, so we went back and crawled inside, trying to fall asleep as quickly as possible, since there weren't many hours left before we had to get up again.

We woke in a pool of water. I thought in a moment of panic that I had wet the bed, something I had done until the age of ten. My parents had been very patient with me, but it was torture. I couldn't ever stay over at friends' houses, and I didn't want to admit why. Finally I stopped. Maybe it was the beginning of puberty, or getting through my parents' second divorce, but eventually I forgot about it until a moment like this, when my first instinct was still one of shame.

It was hard to get out of our wet sleeping bags, which had at least been warmed by our bodies, but by the gray light outside we knew it was past dawn, and it was still raining. Crushing everything together into wet balls of nylon, we made our way to the pavilion and found Sandy Bradley and the crew from The Rubber Chicken just back from the site of the accident. They were standing around under the pavilion, talking in whispers, surrounded by sleeping bodies lying underneath and on top of the picnic tables—refugees from the tents that couldn't stay dry. Max was smoking a cigarette, something I had never seen him do before.

The accident shook everybody up. The Rubber Chicken wasn't the only vehicle we were pushing to the limit. The truck that pulled the stage trailer couldn't go over forty miles an hour in the mountains, and the trailer itself had no brakes. There simply wasn't the money to buy new vehicles of the necessary size and strength. The odds in favor of a real disaster were starting to go up. People complained and worried, but the fact was that the whole Chautauqua was walking that thin line between luck and fate called penury. These were the vehicles we were stuck with, and they still had to go a long way to make it through the tour.

It took most of the morning to get things straightened out with The Rubber Chicken. We hired a wrecker to tow it into Missoula, and the food was distributed among the other vehicles so that we would have some kind of kitchen at our next campsite. Dmitri was driving The Scenicruiser, and I sat behind him until our first stop, which was set for Flathead Lake, Montana. It was a hot day, and the kids changed into their bathing suits hours ahead of time. So much had happened since dawn that it felt strange to begin the journey into Montana now.

Ayla, Alex's daughter, decided she was my child for the day. Her mother had put her on board The Scenicruiser by herself while she went in one of the other vehicles to try to improvise a dinner without the cook bus. Ayla, five years old, with wide blue eyes and straight brown hair cut in bangs, was a sort of *enfant sauvage*. She never wore shoes, and, unsupervised much of the time, she was utterly fearless, throwing herself at trees to climb and banks of dirt to run down at top speed. She was the kind of child who spat on a skinned knee instead of running to her mother. She came up to me on the bus and asked me if I knew why the mountains go up and down. No, I answered truthfully. Because God is sewing the land together, she told me.

The land did look sewn together; the mountains were on all sides, and the highway twisted and turned. On the upper deck of The Scenicruiser, the kids pressed their faces against the tinted glass and squealed as the bus swayed around the corners. We counted mountain goats, who leaped above us at impossible angles.

When we pulled into a gas station, I picked up a paper and learned that Laurence Olivier had died. In fact, he had been dead for three days. I was shocked, not because of his death—he was, after all, an old man—but because I was so far out of touch. This was already old news, relegated to the inner sections of the paper. It could have been months before I found out casually, in the course of a conversation, that he had died, or that there had been a nuclear strike in lower Manhattan. I bought a copy of *People* magazine because his picture was on the cover.

Flathead Lake, fed by glaciers, was the cold turquoise blue that one sees in the eyes of Siberian huskies. Dmitri and I raced each other to the opposite shore of a small inlet. He won, his long arms pulling him easily through the water. We crawled up onto the bank and lay on the pebbled beach like lizards. I had my head in the small of his back, breathing hard from the race. He stretched his legs, pointed his toes, and looked down critically at his torso.

"I used to be on the swim team in high school," he said. "I used to love to race . . ."

I laughed. "We didn't have swimming teams in New York. I learned to swim in the ocean off Cape Cod when I was a kid. We used to go there in the summertime to visit my grandparents. My grandfather had a rule that we kids had to wear life preservers every time we went swimming off the dock until we were old enough to swim all the way across the cove in front of their house. A huge distance to a child. I hated the rule. I was a good swimmer—totally fearless in the ocean—but I was scared of the other side of the cove. The inlet was dark and still, with eel grass growing up from the bottom that I just barely touched with my feet as I swam. So I had to put on this heavy, awful life preserver that made it impossible to dive and float.

"Every summer our grandfather would ask who was ready to take the test. I was the youngest of our pack of five girl cousins, and I watched the older ones make it across by the age of eleven or so. Then they were free of the life preserver, and they dove gracefully off the end of the dock. I envied them, never wanting to be left behind. I was a tomboy like Ayla, and I thought I could do anything. I told my grandfather I was ready to try when I was only eight years old. My sister and my cousins were shocked.

My grandfather just looked at me with an expression that gave nothing away and got into the boat, which he always rowed alongside whichever cousin was swimming.

"I had on my new suit, a one-piece with blue stripes, and I left the life preserver on the dock. My three cousins and my sister all sat on the edge of the dock to watch.

" 'One, two, three . . . go!' my grandfather commanded in his naval-officer's voice. He had served in the Pacific during World War II and had almost been killed when a kamikaze plane hit the deck of his aircraft carrier; he had just left the room to take a pee when the plane hit. Everyone else who had been in the room was killed.

"I dove in, trying to get as much distance from the dock as possible. Then I began to do the crawl, hand over hand, toward the other side. My aim wasn't very good, and I wove back and forth a lot. I looked up, dog-paddled for a few minutes to correct my course, and then pressed on with the crawl. The oars from my grandfather's boat splashed the water next to my head. I didn't look at the boat, only at the other side.

"Halfway across I was so tired that I couldn't lift my arms anymore. The eel grass pulled at my feet, and I was gulping water and spitting it out with every stroke. I wouldn't stop, though, and kept thrashing in the water, going nowhere and getting more and more exhausted. My grandfather stopped rowing altogether and just drifted nearby, watching. He eventually grabbed me by the back of my bathing suit and tossed me onto the bottom of the boat like a puppy. I huddled on the seat in the stern as he rowed back to the dock. Neither of us said a word. He stared past me over my head as he rowed, and I shivered with hate."

"What happened then?" Dmitri hadn't moved for such a long time that I thought he was asleep.

"I had to wear a life preserver for one more year. Then my grandfather died of cancer, and we stopped going to Cape Cod."

. . .

Chewing Blackbones campground, where the Chautauqua finally landed that day, was on a river in a park preserve of the Blackfoot reservation in Montana, which borders Glacier National Park, one of the most dramatic national parks in America. There are glaciers and wild animals spilling over the spine of the Rocky Mountains, which reaches up over the border into Canada. The Blackfoot tribe was edged out of the most scenic areas, however, and we were in a patch of forest at the edge of a dry, barren plain. In the middle of the plain was Browning, Montana, where most of the tribe now lived. The Chautauqua had been here before, and Dmitri had a strong connection with one of the Blackfoot medicine men.

On other visits, the Chautauqua had done a traditional Indian "sweat" with members of the tribe. Sweats, which are like a Native American sauna, take place in small huts, usually near a river. Rocks are heated and placed in the center, and the participants get unbearably hot and then plunge into the water or open the door flap for air. It is a spiritual as well as a physical experience, and prayers are offered up as each stage of the sweat is gone through.

This year the medicine man was gone, and Dmitri was at a loss as to how to connect with the tribe. The show had been advertised (it was a free show, since this was a very poor community), and all of the Chautauquans kept coming up to ask Dmitri about doing a sweat or having a meal with the tribe. He didn't know what to tell them.

It was hot everywhere at our campsite except at the edge of the river, which was banked by trees that looked small in comparison to the huge firs we had seen in the Idaho mountains. We had a quick cold supper, since the cook bus was still in the shop, and someone built a campfire. There was to be a Circle tonight. Susan had hung a small velvet bag with an embroidered design from a tree near the fire. Once we all gathered, she took it down and told us that this was to be a talisman bag for the journey. It would be passed around, and everyone could place in the bag an object or a piece of paper with some words on it, and the bag would be a symbol of our wishes at this moment for the journey. When the bag came around to me, I took off a ring that had come from China and spoke about the massacre in Tiananmen Square. For days now I hadn't been able to get out of my head that famous image of a man standing in front of a line of tanks. I was feeling frustrated with the self-contained world of Chautauqua and wanted to think on a global level, at least for a moment.

The simplification of life on Chautauqua was a relief in some ways, but it also felt like escapism. One didn't have to make decisions about where to go or even what to have for the next meal. The question was whether this simplification allowed larger issues to come up or simply

encouraged people to slip into a sort of mental somnambulism while their physical bodies were pushed to the limit.
It seemed to me such a narrow view of the world, without
The New York Times and CNN to check in with, and I was
even more bothered by the fact that no one else seemed
to care much about the absence of news. Nobody ever
talked politics, and I wondered if some of the people even
knew what I was referring to when I mentioned China.

After the bag was passed around, someone brought up
logistics, but there was an immediate rebellion by the
people who wanted this to be a purely spiritual gathering.
Arguing about whether something was to be a spiritual time
or not proved to be the antithesis of allowing anything
spiritual to happen in any kind of organic way, and the
Circle dispersed, unresolved on every issue except that
people needed to get some sleep.

Dmitri and I set up camp in the darkness next to the
river and built a small campfire of our own in front of the
tent. Benjamin came by and shared Dmitri's special flask
of whiskey that he had brought from Edinburgh years before. It went down hot and sweet, and we didn't talk much.
Nothing mattered more than watching the fire, and the
furthest future was the next day. Later, Dmitri and I made
love next to the fire, a circle of coals no longer hot, and
our breath came out in clouds of white mist.

Ivan dubbed our parade in Browning "The Arena of
Caucasian Humiliation," and that's what it felt like. The
temperature had climbed into the nineties by the middle
of the day, and Browning looked like a third-world town
with everything shuttered and closed down for the midday

siesta. We lined up at the top of the main street with our banners and costumes, just as we always did, and when Ivan gave the signal, we began the parade. Nobody came out to watch. A few pickup trucks drove down the opposite side of the street, and the people inside stared at us impassively. I wondered how many faces were peeking behind the shutters and where the children were. The Chautauqua kids kept asking, "Where is everybody?" and it was at once sad and funny as we kept on marching, playing louder and blowing more bubbles the less response we got. It takes a lot of solidarity to ignore a thirty-piece marching band, and as we all piled back onto the bus when the parade was over, I wondered about bringing entertainment to the "underprivileged." Was it more for our benefit than theirs?

The stage site was a huge field ringed by evergreens near our campsite. Black-eyed Susans grew tough and tall out of the sharp grass, which was mined with cow pats. Worse than those were the black flies that bit everybody the moment they started to sweat. Allen and I took turns driving the shovel into the hard ground for the trapeze. With the heat, we could work only in short spurts, and the stage crew complained steadily as they raised the lighting truss. The band canceled its rehearsal after Joe Watts, the drummer from L.A., who wasn't too crazy about camping to begin with, refused to put up with the flies any longer. Nobody in the band gave him much of an argument.

Allen and I didn't have a choice; the trapeze had to be up by show time, and it would take at least a couple of hours. Dmitri had disappeared ever since the parade.

He had found a phone booth and was trying to keep in touch with New York and L.A. via his various answering machines. "No, you can't call me back, I'm at a phone booth in Montana . . ." I knew he would also be trying to call Anita, at home.

Two hours later, Allen and I were the last ones left at the site, doing final touches on the trapeze rig. The empty stage sat hot and black in the sun, with rows of folding chairs for the band sitting empty next to it. The brightly colored flags that made the bunting for the front of the stage flapped slowly back and forth, and as soon as the last of the ropes was tightened down, Allen and I ran for the shade of the campsite.

I avoided the main camp area. I was too hot to socialize, so I went straight to our tent, stripped down, and stepped into the stream. It came up only to my ankles, but I squatted and splashed the icy water all over my body. The fly bites were already coming up in ugly red welts on my skin. I could hear Benjamin playing his cheap beater guitar which he took on the road. Angela had ended up camping in Psycho Car again. I could tell she was running out of energy for camping. She had sat next to me at the Circle last night, but we hadn't seen each other alone for days, and I missed her. I saw Dmitri come walking up the road from the main camp, swatting flies, and I wrapped myself up in a towel and ducked inside the tent, wanting to surprise him. Instead of coming over to the tent, however, he squatted outside, poking at the remains of our campfire with a stick. I crawled up to the mosquito netting and watched him. He must have known I was there, but he didn't turn, and I said nothing. All of the flirtation dropped out of me in a rush, and I pulled the towel tighter.

Before he looked over at me I knew he was crying. I couldn't decide whether to go to him or not and waited at the front of the tent for some sign. He started talking all at once, his hands cupping each other, pushing the stick hard into the dirt. Anita had been home, working in the garden. For some reason that stuck with me. Of course she had a garden there, a life, her teenage son was there with her. The phone had rung. She must have been thinking every time it rang that it might be him—and this time it was—and all of the fantasies that everything would be all right were banished from that moment on. I could feel it as if it were inside my own bones: the collapse inward that comes with the certainty of knowing that the worst is actually happening right now. No more rationalizations, no more wild hopes.

I suppose I had thought that I would feel more relief than I did that he had finally confirmed what she already knew, and now we were out of the gray area and into the open, where everything stood out in black and white. But there was no relief, just the fact of being on the other side of that moment of confrontation. Being on the other side meant that anything could happen to us now, and I watched him, wanting to comfort him across a vast territory of grief. I couldn't ever know what intimacies and cruelties he was mourning.

He wanted to walk but still to have me there with him, so I followed him upstream, away from the campsite, keeping a bit of distance. The landscape was full of destruction.

Great trees lay uprooted across the streambed, their root systems leaving gaping holes in the banks. The stream was shallow and broken up by gravel bars, which silted up the stream to one side or another as the water pushed against them. The scale of everything seemed so huge that afternoon; the mountains hunched over us indifferently.

Dmitri had been talking with Ivan and his wife the day before about where things stood with Anita. A lot was thrown into question: for one thing, what would happen with the bed-and-breakfast business if she left the house immediately. He had to make peace with his partners and extended family without knowing if there would ever be peace with her. I listened, not knowing what advice to give him about the twenty-year-old politics of his vaudeville family, where everyone's actions ricocheted off everyone else.

When the logs became too jammed to keep walking upstream, we turned and climbed the bank into a cow pasture. Holding hands now, we walked back down along the river, and he asked me if I could sing to the cows as Rebo had done once in Ireland, drawing them close and quiet with her voice. I tried, but I was tired of ex-wives and girlfriends, and my voice would never be as sweet as Rebo's. The cows were uninterested, and I hated myself for letting a herd of cows hurt my feelings. Back at camp, someone had filled vases with flowers and placed them on the picnic tables where we ate. It was the nicest thing that happened in Browning.

The show that night became a drive-in. The local people, members of the Blackfoot tribe, chose to stay in their cars, a fair distance from the stage. It was eerie, as darkness came on, to be playing to a row of silent pickup trucks behind the ten or twenty people who dared to get closer to live entertainment. I kept expecting someone to pull out a .22 rifle and start shooting when he didn't like the act. The show, in response to this, got loose and crazy, which made it more fun for us, but the audience didn't react. Afterward a tribal leader came up to Dmitri and gave him a braid of sweet grass and some Indian tobacco in thanks, but almost everyone else vanished as soon as the finale was over.

I lay awake for a long time that night, listening to Dmitri's breathing and wondering why there are such long stretches of time when nothing changes and everything seems desperately stuck; then everything happens all at once and nothing is ever the same.

CHAPTER
7

JUST BEFORE ENTERING Glacier National Park, Angela stopped Psycho Car in the small town of St. Mary. Angela, Joe Watts, Dmitri, and I were riding together to our next stop, in Sandpoint, Idaho. Angela had wanted me to reunite with her in Psycho Car for quite a while now, and since Dmitri and I were, as she put it, "joined at the hip," she said he could come along as well. If she was hoping that I would say no and insist that she and I do the long drive alone, as we had to Boise, I disappointed her. I wanted to be with Dmitri all the time now. Joe Watts must have seen what he thought would be a fun ride, so he came, too, folding his long legs into the front seat while Dmitri and I shared the back with Angela's clothes and saxophone case.

We found a store where we could buy snacks for the trip, but I didn't bother to buy extra film for my camera. Though Glacier is one of the most dramatic of all the national parks, with lots of wildlife, we were going to drive on the main road, and I doubted we would see anything more than squirrels. If I wanted to see wildlife I would rent a nature video. In the store, Dmitri and I got to talking with the salesgirl, who told us about Angus Black. He had opened a bar in St. Mary many years ago, and he let any tribe member have a tab at the bar. When it came time to pay up, he took back the debt from them in land. By now Angus Black owned almost all of the town and surrounding area, right up to the border of the national park. Dmitri and I must have looked stunned by this story, for the salesgirl called out cheerily as we headed for the door, "But don't let it bum you out, man."

We drove along the well-paved road of the park, eating black licorice and counting the RVs that lined the road, each surrounded by overwrought children in Day-Glo colors. There was water everywhere, streams and waterfalls on the side of the road and views of snow-peaked mountains and flower-covered glacier fields. We had left the members of the Blackfoot tribe behind the windshields of their pickup trucks on the outskirts of Browning, a dusty town that wasn't on the RV trail.

Once on the other side of the park, we pressed on, back into the northern finger of Idaho, which reaches up like a peninsula between Montana and eastern Washington.

We were heading toward Sandpoint, Idaho, where we were to perform that night in an old vaudeville house that had been converted into a movie theatre but was ready to welcome us onto its narrow stage as the first vaudevillians to have tread those boards since the talkies were invented.

It was midafternoon by the time the whole troupe arrived to set up for an eight o'clock show, although, since we were playing inside, all we really had to do was set the lights and hang a banner at the back of the stage. The theatre had almost no wings. An old strip of footlights stared up at us with empty sockets. The ceiling was high enough to hang a trapeze, but layers of black velvet masked the proscenium, which meant that, although I could hang my trapeze from the gridwork on the ceiling, the part of my routine that took place above the bar would be blocked. After talking it over with Allen, I decided to modify my routine to whatever I had worked out below the bar and to shorten the act by about a minute. We rigged the trapeze, and I climbed up to the bar to work out the new routine while the band practiced in the parking lot.

It was peaceful and solitary hanging from the bar by my ankles as the music drifted in through the stage door. I did some slow pull-ups for conditioning while the stage crew worked below me, largely unaware of my presence. Occasionally there would be a pause in the music, and I could hear Ivan giving directions to the players. Then the drums and the horns would start up again. I didn't mind hearing the same song over and over again, because time had paused for me that afternoon, sitting in the air above the dark stage.

But the day began to pick up momentum, as show days always do. We had arrived late after the long drive, and soon I found myself eating a quick dinner off the trestle tables set up next to The Rubber Chicken in the parking lot behind the theatre. Then it was time to go. The band formed up behind the theatre and marched around the corner of the building and in from the back of the house, scattering the local children who had been peering at us from a safe distance.

The house was packed, with people standing at the back and sitting in the aisles. About halfway through the first act, the local fire marshal appeared and brought everything to a halt as he insisted on clearing the aisles. Pop Wagner, a lariat twirler and folksinger who had joined up with the Chautauqua just that day, was doing his act for the first time when the fire department arrived. He thought it was a joke that the Chautauquans were playing on him, a kind of "hazing" because it was his first show. The marshal was standing to the side, next to the band. He had given the word to Dmitri, who had passed it on to Pop.

"You can't just stop the show, like that," Pop said to Dmitri, still twirling his lariat.

"It's not me. Talk to him, he's the fire marshal." Dmitri pointed the man out with his clarinet.

"You're the fire marshal? Where's your uniform?" Pop was now jumping in and out of the loop.

"It's at home." This got a big laugh, and the fire marshal floundered, very embarrassed to have the entire audience waiting for his response. "But I am the fire marshal, everybody knows that. You've got to clear all of these people out of the aisles. It's a safety hazard."

"But how can I clear the aisles?" asked Pop. "I'm up here doing a show."

"All I know is that these aisles have to be cleared, now," the fire marshal said, in what sounded like his best "bad cop" voice. Nobody moved.

"You see, that would be much more effective if you had your uniform on," Pop said, still doing rope tricks. "I wear this big white hat and boots and chaps so that people will *know* I'm a cowboy. It's an image thing. Image is very important if you're a public person like you and I."

"I am *not* a public person!" The fire marshal was blushing.

"Hold on, hold on, I'm about to give you your chance." Pop stopped spinning his rope, and it settled back onto his arm, just an ordinary rope, all illusion gone. He beckoned to the fire marshal. "I would like to invite you to be my brave volunteer." The crowd roared. The fire marshal stared at Pop in terror.

"Come on," Pop said to him in a stage whisper. "It's my big finish. Don't blow it for me, sir."

The fire marshal turned to Dmitri, who he mistakenly thought was in charge, but Dmitri was laughing along with everybody else. The fire marshal looked back at Pop and then out at the crowd. It was a small town; he must have known everybody out there.

"Okay," he said, getting up onto the stage. "But only after the aisles have been cleared."

So a compromise was reached. Pop stopped his act long enough for the fire marshal to get the people sitting in the aisles to move to the back of the theatre, and then Pop used the fire marshal as a volunteer. He dropped a rope over his head and twirled the lariat down around his body. Usually he did this part of the act with children, so he had to stand on a chair to be able to drop a rope over the marshal.

The dialogue between Pop and the fire marshal at the back of the theatre outdid the act itself. The audience loved the whole thing; it was one of those towns where everybody knew everybody else and everyone had an opinion about the fire department.

The show went on for over three hours, and we got a standing ovation at the end. The tear-down was faster than usual with no stage or trapeze to take down and pack into the trailer. We were staying the night with the "Hooey Man," a tall, quiet man who made little wooden toys called "hooeys," small sticks with several notches cut into them and a small wooden propeller on the end. As you rubbed a stick back and forth along the notches, the propeller spun. The Hooey Man and his wife didn't have a lot of land, but they fired up their sauna and strung the woods with Christmas lights. They were happy to let us camp on the hillside above their trailer, and almost everyone stopped in at the sauna.

The Hooey Man had a son about twelve years old, who was fast on the way to becoming as much of an expert on the spoons as Artis the Spoonman himself. The boy had gone on Chautauqua several summers before as a protégé of Artis's, but the summer I met him he was wearing heavy metal T-shirts and looked like a sixteen-year-old. He lurked around the group that night, eyeing the two teenage girls who were with us, but they were too hip to give him a second glance. The pair, both beauties, one blond and one dark, rode with Artis because he had the best music. Artis always kept up with them, too; his collection of heavy metal and punk music was impressive for a grandfather.

The next morning, all of the vehicles were miraculously on the road by 6:45 A.M. Dmitri and I were in the grain truck that pulled the stage trailer, and he and Ivan recited a Hebrew prayer for safe travel over the CB. We needed travel prayers that day. It was going to be a long haul to Omak, in eastern Washington, and the grain truck groaned as it started out. Not many people were entrusted with driving the grain truck; it was one of the older vehicles. After Max's experience with The Rubber Chicken, Dmitri had been pressured to take over the truck from the other designated drivers, who had been complaining about handling the beast ever since Chautauqua began. It was a big, heavy truck with loose steering and uncertain brakes. The stage trailer, which had no brakes of its own, was completely dependent on the truck to slow it down on the hills. Dmitri had been driving large, uncertain vehicles for most of his life, and I trusted him. In fact, the two of us loved driving the grain truck in spite of the risk and the slow pace we were forced to go, because for us it meant privacy. The cab was noisy but roomy, with old vinyl seats that were wide enough for me to lie down comfortably with my head in Dmitri's lap as he drove. I stuck my bare feet out the window and studied the chips on my red toenail polish.

We had bought a copy of William Shirer's *Berlin Diary* at a second-hand bookstore in Sandpoint, and I read it out loud as we drove. It was strange to be reading about pre–World War II Germany while we were passing acres of wheat fields toward the Grand Coulee Dam. The scenery had the unreality of an advertisement for the plenitude of America. Everything seemed to have a golden wash of light over it as the morning wore on to midday. Occasional flocks of blackbirds started up out of the fields when we rattled by, and I would be shocked out of my train of thought and unaware that I had stopped reading until Dmitri nudged me to start up again.

It had been so long since I had seen a horizon so wide and flat that I didn't mind going slow. The day had one of those skies that are more white than blue, and the bright yellow of the fields made it seem as if the sun were shining up from the ground to the sky. We were now the slowest vehicle and the last in the caravan. Only The Rubber Chicken stayed within range of our CB, the theory being that if one of the vehicles had trouble, the other would be close enough to help out.

Over a gentle hill that looked like every other one, the Grand Coulee Dam broke smoothly into the landscape ahead. Its presence had been announced to us again and again by neatly lettered highway signs, but none of them had told us the size of it. Such a huge mass of concrete in the midst of all those fields which were hardly even moored by houses. The great Columbia River, which grew wider and wider until it finally met the sea in Oregon, was transformed into a small ribbon of water by the enormous concrete harness that came down over it as soon as it crossed the border from Canada. Does a river carry memories with it of a cold mountain stream in British Columbia?

As we approached the dam, we saw two school buses pulled over to the side of the road. Of course they were ours, and one of them had a decided tilt to the starboard. It was The Nimbus, Artis's dark orange hulk, and The Rubber Chicken was pulled up behind it. We drove the truck and trailer in behind them, and I imagined the tourists' faces pressed up tight against the tinted glass of the circular "convenience center" located nearby. I decided that more of them were probably watching us than were watching the dam, as more and more people in T-shirts and ponytails came pouring out of the vehicles.

The Nimbus had a flat tire. Artis had a spare but not a jack that was strong enough to raise the weight of the bus. We searched The Rubber Chicken, which was also ill-equipped for a flat. The grain truck had a jack, which we discussed at length, but in the end we decided that it would never work for The Nimbus.

As everyone went over and over the endless possibilities, I walked to the dam with Nick, a sophisticated twelve-year-old who was full of wise-ass remarks and flirtation. I had been a cocky kid myself, so Nick and I formed an immediate friendship. He played saxophone in the band, while his father, a gentle man with the handsome furrowed face of a sailor, played the piccolo. Nick and I got as close as we could to the dam without jumping the fence that prevented anyone from actually walking out to the middle and looking down, which, of course, is exactly what we wanted to do. We were able to get right next to it, however, and it stretched down for what looked like miles of slick gray concrete.

I had been to the locks of the Panama Canal earlier that year, on a trip with my father, who was there on a journalistic assignment, and the authorities had let us walk across the dam. I had even been given the thrill of moving the levers that controlled the locks, and I had felt the same wonder at American engineering that I did now. A small plaque commemorating the Army Corps of Engineers was all that was bolted to the canal in Panama, a plaque that told nothing of the dead Chinese and West Indian laborers who broke through that wet earth and succumbed to malaria, climate, and disease; or of those who in fact had the practical knowledge of how to break through a mountain and control the flow of water between two of the world's greatest seas. I didn't know the story of this dam, but I knew that it was built when the dust bowls were whirling across the land and the wheat fields were brown with drought, and to be working on the dam was to be counted lucky because it was a job. "The U.S. Army Corps of Engineers," read a small plaque near the dam. Once again, it told us nothing.

When we returned to the vehicles, we found out that the highway patrol had been called, and Artis was firing up espresso for everybody on his stove. He didn't seem too worried. The teenage girls had volunteered to stay behind with him; they knew where the party was, even if the party vehicle was temporarily out of service.

Meanwhile, The Rubber Chicken and the grain truck lumbered on. We were carrying the kitchen and the stage, both of which had to be set up that night. Eventually we left the plains for the eastern foothills of the Cascade mountain range, which divides Washington and Oregon roughly into thirds, the smallest portion being on the coast. There are four live volcanoes in this range, including Mount St. Helen's, which erupted in 1980, throwing ash for miles and literally blowing the top off the mountain. I remember driving past the mountain on the interstate not long afterward and seeing the gray line of mud like a high-tide mark on the trees. It was spring, but the dying leaves had changed to fall colors, and the mountainside was covered with trees that had landed haphazardly, like a spilled box of wooden matches. Mount Rainier, Mount Hood, and Mount Baker, the other giants of this range, gave off puffs of white smoke from time to time, which made me wonder.

As we climbed higher into the Cascades, the land turned to scrub, and the weather got cold. Everything was etched in shades of black and white. Granite showed through the dirt, and the road was cracked and rough. It had the feeling of wintertime even though it was still midsummer. Alex and I had discovered a mutual love of Rilke, and she had loaned me a volume of poems she had brought with her. I switched from *Berlin Diary* to Rilke and read aloud passages about angels as we drove through that bitter landscape.

Dmitri and I were scheduled to make dinner that night, and of course we were the last to arrive in Omak. Night had fallen suddenly, as it does in the mountains, and the empty stalls of farm animals at the county fairgrounds where we were camping loomed in the dark. Angela and Faith joined us in the kitchen as we lit candles, opened a bottle of wine, and began to cook dinner for forty. Dmitri, Angela, and I started to have a loud argument in mock Italian as we decided that when Dmitri and I were cooking, the Rubber Chicken was "Paolo and Francesca's Ristorante Italiano" and Angela owned our competition, "Milo's," across the street. We had shopped for a special Sephardic fish recipe Dmitri had learned from his family of Spanish Jews. Faith got bored with our Italian arguments and began to talk about God, challenging Dmitri to define his Judaism.

"Come on, Dmitri," she said. "In the old days you called yourself a pagan. Weren't you even some kind of Druid for a while, in California?"

"No. I was never a pagan," he said. "I never went away from Judaism. I practice more than anyone else in my family does, now."

"Even your mother?" Angela grinned at him.

"Even my mother. She doesn't do Shabbat every Friday like I do."

"But you travel and work on the sabbath. That's not doing it right, is it?" I asked. Practically everyone I had grown up with in New York was Jewish, and though none of their families practiced, I knew some of the rules.

Dmitri stopped chopping vegetables and looked at me without smiling. "I know. I wish I could do it right. But I'm in show business." He spoke quietly.

I was shocked. Being religious was not anything I had ever known about him, and it made me uncomfortable.

"You see," he went on after a pause, "the whole idea is that everyone has this spark of divine energy in them. There's an old rabbinic tale of the creation which tells about the world being contained in a clay pot, and when it was broken, all of the sparks of divine energy escaped and flew to all different parts of the world. Each person has that spark inside of him. The Jews believe that if for one Sabbath—only one—every Jew kept the Sabbath as they're supposed to, the Messiah would come."

"Oh, come on." Angela poured more wine for everybody. "Do you really believe in the Messiah? The nuns beat that out of me long ago."

"Well, you can think of it either as a person or the Messianic age. An age of peace and enlightenment. I mean, isn't that what we're all striving for anyway? Why donate your time to go on Chautauqua? I'm not kidding at the end of every show when I tell the audience to go out there and save the world."

"But can you save the world by staying home once a week and not driving, or using electric lights, or all of those other crazy rules?" I asked.

Dmitri smiled. "We won't know until it happens."

"Maybe that's the brilliance of the concept," Faith said, pushing a lock of gray hair back up under her scarf as she chopped more garlic. "It would be impossible to get that many people to do the same thing for one day, so that's why the Messiah hasn't come."

Dmitri laughed. "Maybe. But if they ever did, you never know what might happen."

"Yeah, but what about once the Messiah comes, then

what?" Angela leaned her chin on my shoulder and stared provocatively at Dmitri. "We all sit around playing harps and having a love fest? How boring."

I laughed. "Yeah. I think I'm too much of a New Yorker for that myself."

"You won't know if it's boring 'til it happens," Dmitri said, tasting the cream sauce. "Dinner is served."

Faith leaned out of the door and banged on a pot. "Dinner! Come and get it while it's hot!" she yelled.

The fish floated in a creamy lemon sauce, and we served wine and ate off the trestle tables by candlelight. The weather had gotten colder, and it was late, but people sat up talking after dinner until Pop Wagner was persuaded to do his flaming lariat trick on top of the bus. He climbed up to the roof of The Rubber Chicken—cowboy boots and hat in place as always—dipped the rope in white gas, and lit it. He spun the flaming cord over his head and then dropped it around his waist, still spinning. The flames lit up his compact form. We shouted like children for him to do it again and again, and he obliged us. Spinning hoops of fire over the encampment until it got too cold for his hands to twirl the rope and all of the candles had burned black circles into the table tops.

The next morning we broke camp early and drove to the show site in Omak: a small green field near the Breadline Cafe, a large seventies-style restaurant run by ex-hippies who were our sponsors in town. They provided us with a huge brunch and a place to hold our logistical meeting, which was scheduled for the morning. The idea was that we would get over the Canadian border that night, packing up and leaving after the show. It would be an incredible push to get there, but the feeling was that we might not be searched so thoroughly at night. No one was supposed to be carrying anything illegal in any case, but the idea of a customs officer going through all of the props, costumes, and personal items of the troupe was a nightmare for everybody.

Our destination was Quadra Island, a small island off the coast of Vancouver Island, which is a long finger of an island with a huge mountain range that towers over the strait across from Vancouver, Canada. The Chautauqua had been there several times before and had always had a good welcome from the community. Crossing the border, however, was a logistical nightmare that put everyone on the honor system; there was a new law that enabled the government to seize a vehicle if they found so much as a seed of marijuana aboard. The Karamazovs could ill afford to lose their touring bus, the Scenicruiser, over someone's stash. After the meeting, everyone was ordered to go and get his or her personal belongings and look through them carefully. Then the belongings were to be tagged with special fluorescent tape that Fyodor Karamazov (he seemed to be overseeing this operation) gave out. He wanted to be in charge of the final loading of the bus, to be absolutely sure that, once everything was taken off, it would not be put back on board until it was tagged as clean.

Allen, my rigger, wasn't going to Canada because he didn't want to risk it with his vehicle. Maybe he didn't want to stop smoking pot for that long as well. We were going to be up there for three days. I wished he would change his mind. Now I had to learn how to rig the trapeze by myself—with Dmitri's and Orbit's help. Orbit was a tall hippie who ran the juggling workshops with Ivan's wife and was my other spotter during the act. I was very nervous about putting up the trapeze without Allen; even though I had been involved in every step of the operation, he had been the mastermind.

After the meeting broke up, everyone else went to check their bags, and Dmitri and I went to learn the set-up from Allen. I wrote everything down, even what I already knew—making notes and drawing a chart in my notebook. The lowering or raising of the rig was the most frightening part. I was always sure that a cable would snap or one of the big stakes would pull out of the soft earth, sending those two huge poles crashing to the ground. I didn't want full responsibility for the rigging, but Allen only smiled his crooked smile that made him look like a pirate when I begged him to come along. He knew I wasn't joking, and I knew he wasn't coming along. He would meet us at the next gig on this side of the border, up in the San Juan Islands.

Someone had brought a white horse for Pop Wagner to ride in the parade. It was a big horse with Western-style tack and a braided mane. Pop asked me to walk beside him as he did lariat tricks from the saddle. He wanted to twirl the rope around me as he rode. It was the best thing I could think of doing in the parade, short of riding the horse myself.

There wasn't much to Main Street in Omak: a hardware store, a cafe, a tavern, a grain supply store, and three beauty shops. There always seem to be a lot of beauty shops in small towns. Maybe it is the business that every town needs most: the manicures, the pedicures, the gossip. The street was wide, and the buildings were white and spread out evenly on either side of the street. One got the feeling there was plenty of space in this town, and the buildings didn't rub up against each other the way they did back east. Unlike Browning, people seemed to want us here. They came out to stand in their doorways and waved to us as we paraded past. Some even joined in the parade. They were also mainly white people in Omak, and for all I knew these were the neo-Nazis who were happily waving as we went by.

We ended up back at the show site with lots of strangers in tow, and the band cut loose. They jammed on Beatles songs and strange selections from Fellini movies. They could go from "Mellow Yellow" to the theme from *Black Orpheus* in the blink of an eye. Pop and I posed for pictures with the horse until the band stopped playing and the crowd slowly drifted off. The horse's owner, a ten-year-old girl who had walked with us, holding the reins, said goodbye and climbed onto the horse's back as if she were going up a staircase. She looked very plain in her blue jeans and T-shirt with her horse all dressed up for the parade.

Actually, she looked just like a ten-year-old who owned such a magnificent horse should look. She had been the one to braid his mane early that morning in the barn. She had been the one who had polished his saddle and bridle, not even bothering to wash her own hands before bringing him over. I had hardly spoken to her during the parade.

She had been totally concentrated on the horse, speaking to him quietly as Pop twirled his lariat and occasionally brushed the side of the horse's neck with the rope. I liked her without knowing her. She reminded me of Tina.

Tina was one of my best friends from second grade until eighth grade. Her parents had a country house north of the city, and I spent every weekend with them for years. At fourteen she went away to school, and puberty broke us apart for a few years. When we met again on the other side of adolescence, we became friends again. Much had changed, but we were both essentially the same. Tina had three sisters, all younger, and she and I shared a passionate love of dogs first, then horses. We both had dogs—hers was a Brittany spaniel and mine was a mutt with some Shetland sheepdog mixed in. One summer day we rode our bikes for miles on the country roads around her house, putting flyers we had made into every mailbox, announcing our dog show. We were going to hold it in her driveway. The only class to be judged was obedience.

Finally the day of the dog show arrived. We had made a banner to go over the driveway so that people could find it easily, but we were the only ones there. Tina's father, a tall, angular man with a great talent for telling ghost stories, came out and gravely judged our two dogs against each other. I don't know how he managed it, but he was very diplomatic, and we both came away feeling good about our dogs' results. Perhaps he created separate categories for them: mutts and purebreds. I remember the two of us being surprised but not crushed at the poor showing for our event. Maybe we were secretly grateful for the lack of competition, which left our dogs on top, as we knew they deserved to be.

Tina's parents rented horses for several summers, fencing off a field below the house as a pasture. They had a pinto pony, who was ornery and stubborn, a medium-sized horse, who was steady, and a larger one, who was glorious and took some handling. I usually rode the pinto, named Sancho Panza, and Tina rode the medium-sized horse. It seemed appropriate since she was more experienced at riding and definitely the ringleader in this department— my Don Quixote. Being the oldest children, we were allowed to take off on our own.

On hot days we wore only our high-waisted cotton underpants and painted the rest of our bodies with warpaint, which we made from mud and berries. Tina had two long pigtails, which flew out behind her as she rode. She could go faster on her horse than Sancho and I, but Sancho would stand quietly and let me vault him from behind, landing on his bare back with a shriek. We carved arrows and made bows from young saplings so that we could lean low on the necks of our steeds and shoot the arrows off into the brush. They were very patient horses.

Some nights Tina's mother would give us hot dogs, and we would make a fire circle at the far end of the driveway and roast them on sticks in the dark. We always sat facing the woods so that we could pretend there was no civilization for miles, until one of Tina's sisters came out of the house to tell us about a television show that was on—"I Love Lucy" or "Creature Feature"—and we would run back inside to watch, the twentieth century breaking in on us

141

again. Tina would have acted the way the ten-year-old did today. Serious about her work.

Fyodor had pulled everyone's packs and tents from the bus after the meeting, and now he was rushing around like a drill sergeant with his roll of fluorescent tape. Not everyone was ready to mark off their bags as clean and drug-free yet, though I'm sure that if any of them did have drugs they knew exactly where they were keeping them. But Fyodor wanted everyone to double-check, and he was right, of course, so we sat on the lawn pretending to be customs officers and going through the lining of every pocket for contraband. The people who lived in Omak were probably surprised to see the troupe spilling all of their personal belongings out onto the village green. I overheard one local politely asking Rebo exactly how long we were going to be in town. It could have been a party, but everyone was so rushed that it was hard to enjoy ourselves. We still had to have dinner, do a show, tear it down, have a quick meeting to reconnoiter, and then drive about two hundred miles to the border. It was a crazy plan. A Chautauqua plan. There was a joke on this tour, that we *could* do things the easy way—but we would do them the "Chautauqua" way instead.

It got dark before intermission, and I spent most of the show trying to keep my body warmed up before I went on. The routine felt like work that night. I hoped it didn't look like it. Everyone in the show was tired. There was a general dread of what was to come that showed in the performances. Faith and Artis, who both usually ran over their allotted ten minutes, kept it down to seven or eight, and even the Karamazovs basically stayed within their regular patter. Not too many flights of improvisation tonight.

After the show Allen and I tried to get the rig down as quickly as possible, but we were still the last ones to arrive at the "brief" meeting that was to be a prelude to our departure for Canada. The restaurant was once again letting us have the dining room as a meeting place. They had cleared out the tables and chairs, and everyone had drawn into the traditional circle on the floor. The silence that Allen and I walked into was strange, and we both looked around guiltily as we slipped inside the door. Even our footsteps sounded too loud all of a sudden.

Fyodor was speaking. Maybe that was why it was so quiet; no one usually expected him to speak, onstage or off, since he was naturally quiet. But now he was speaking with an intensity that was a little frightening. There was a change of plans. Fyodor had called the border and found out that the crossing we were headed for wouldn't be open as late as we were certain to arrive. So all of the packing and planning had been pointless. For now, there was no point in rushing up to the border; we might as well sleep here and head out as early as possible in the morning. Fyodor was white with anger about changing the plan, and about the group's inefficiency. He was a very economical man. Economical with words and gestures. He kept speaking for several minutes, staring straight ahead, after Allen and I came in. Everyone sat in a circle looking down at their laps or even falling asleep, but certainly not daring to look at Fyodor. The rule at Chautauqua meetings was that no one could be interrupted while they had the floor, and Fyodor didn't seem to want to give it up.

It all seemed to me very pointless and surreal. Sitting in the middle of an empty restaurant at midnight, knowing that we all had to get up in about five hours, and going over and over something that was indeed a mistake, but also at this point merely a fact. Nothing could be done to change it, and everyone clearly wanted to go to bed. When Fyodor eventually stopped speaking, there was a long expectant pause, until Susan remarked that it was very late now, and if we all agreed to be on the road by 6:00 A.M., perhaps we should adjourn this meeting.

Uninterrupted listening with a lack of direct response was something I was to witness over and over again on Chautauqua. Though no one could argue with the rule about not interrupting people when they spoke, what happened in reality was that a mediator made lists of people who wanted to respond, and they would raise their hands to have their names written down in order of request to speak. Unfortunately, by the time you got a chance to speak, the issue you were responding to would be long gone, and in order to give everyone a chance to speak, all of the meeting time was usually used up before any real decisions could be made. It was democracy, but democracy with no possibility of free-flow discussion and response.

I wondered what was supposed to happen in a case like this. One person expressed his justified dissatisfaction, and everyone seemed simply to walk away from it. It felt strange and unresolved to me, but I was just like everyone else, reluctant to confront Fyodor's anger, which had an edge to it. And he was a Karamazov, after all. At this point, almost all anyone was thinking of was sleep, and Susan's statement seemed to give everyone permission to breathe again. The troupe quickly agreed to adjourn, and people began to hoist their sleeping children over their shoulders. The restaurant had told Rebo and Susan that we could sleep in the big room all together, as no one had set up their tents and everything was packed away.

I made my way to Dmitri, who gave me his hand, distracted. We were planning to sleep in the blue room— the big double bed at the back of the bus. Fyodor walked over as we headed for the door and stopped us with a gesture. I felt Dmitri's body stiffen as he turned to Fyodor. He didn't let go of my hand.

"I wanted to sleep in the blue room tonight," Fyodor said after a long pause. He seemed to be having a hard time speaking at all, and he was so tense that I felt an overwhelming feeling of empathy for him. Dmitri wasn't helping him out.

"I put a note up on the door this afternoon," Dmitri said. "Reserving it for Francesca and me." Dmitri had told me he wanted to sleep there for first shift while Fyodor was driving the bus. They had planned to switch off after the first hour. Fyodor breathed heavily, gearing up to speak again. Dmitri just waited.

"What time did you put up the note?" Fyodor asked.

"I don't know what time it was." Dmitri was at the edge of yelling at Fyodor. "Francesca and I are sleeping in the blue room tonight. You want it—you reserve it."

I wanted nothing more than to be gone. This was beyond where we were all going to sleep that night. This had to do with years of history, and I wished more than anything that Dmitri would let go of my hand so that I could step away from their circle of animosity.

Fyodor's eyes got wider, and he stared down and then up at Dmitri again. Dmitri waited for what seemed like a long time. I was totally aware of the fact that everyone else in the room was watching, if only out of the corners of their eyes. Fyodor said nothing, and Dmitri finally turned and walked away. I kept my eyes averted from Dmitri and everyone else as we left the restaurant and headed for The Scenicruiser.

There were sleeping bodies on every bunk as we made our way to the back of the bus. Dmitri slid open the wooden door to the blue room and ripped down the note he had left taped to it.

"When *did* you put the note up?" I asked. I had to.

"I don't know. I guess not early enough for Fyodor."

It was the first time he had snapped at me. We took off our clothes and got into bed in silence. I felt like crying but didn't want to. None of this was about me, after all, and I knew that. But his anger frightened me. We lay in silence for a long time, neither of us sleeping. He turned toward me at last, putting out his arm, which felt heavy, crushing my ribs.

"I'm sorry."

My breath let go, and the tears came all at once. He licked at the corners of my eyes like an animal, and though I turned to him, I felt suddenly, deeply, that I was in the wrong place. My breathing slowed down eventually, and his did, too, until I realized that he had fallen asleep. I lay awake for another hour or more. I knew this place; it was familiar. The time that women spend awake, unable to let go of the beating of their own minds, while men, despite their best efforts, are overcome by sleep. The unknowing desertion that every man is capable of, while women keep a watch through the night.

CHAPTER
8

DMITRI AND I slept in the blue room of The Scenicruiser, but we drove to Canada in the grain truck. Dmitri was up after only three hours of sleep and infuriatingly cheerful. I don't respond well to early-morning cheeriness, and I fell back to sleep almost as soon as we got into the truck. I didn't want coffee because I didn't want to wake up. We were the first vehicle on the road that morning, but it didn't last long. First The Scenicruiser lumbered by, its rear end black with exhaust. Then Magical Mystical Michael drove by in his van, a luxury vehicle equipped with air conditioning and a high-tech sound system. Angela was next in Psycho Car with Rebo

Flordigan and Max. The Rubber Chicken, The Nimbus, and the Mother Hen followed behind in a little pack.

We were traversing a long series of switchbacks up the mountain. The road was narrow, and Dmitri kept having to pull over to the right shoulder to let other vehicles go by. There was mile upon mile of Douglas firs going out in every direction, tall evergreens that let the light just barely leak through their branches. Huge bald patches on the opposite mountainside showed where the forest had been clear-cut. Some of the clear-cuts went on for hundreds of miles: the forest had been razed to the ground without regard for the waste and erosion that followed.

The clear-cuts stopped as suddenly as they began, and driving through the Cascades looked as if someone had been playing Russian roulette with the trees. One never knew which bend in the road might open onto an unexpected patch of land where huge trees lay torn open, the stumps broken off jagged. The bones of the mountainside were exposed in the unaccustomed light. Foxglove and fireweed shot up pink and purple through the wreckage. Then the wall of trees would come up again, and the forest lay moist and dark all around us.

The only store we saw on this side of the pass advertised "Live Bait" and had a small fleet of Harley-Davidson motorcycles in front. We stopped out of boredom. Even if we didn't need gas, we could use the human contact. On the porch of the store was an old boot tied onto what looked like the rusted seat of a tractor. A long arm on a hinge was attached to the boot, and it all ended in a huge, rusty spring, cocked and ready to go. "Self-Kicking Machine" read the sign. For twenty-five cents you could give yourself a kick in the behind if that's what you thought you deserved. We both wanted to try it, of course, but the machine was broken—had been for years. It sat out in front of the store to give it a sense of identity. There were postcards inside: "I got my ass kicked at . . ." and so on.

The boot looked old and mean, as if it might really hurt. It also looked to me like one of Mrs. DeSalle's toy banks. Mrs. DeSalle was an old lady when I met her, the mother of a friend of my father's, who had become his friend as well despite the difference in age. We used to visit her in the country, somewhere north of the city, in Connecticut. The toy banks were intricate little machines cast in lead and brightly painted. You placed a penny in a dog's mouth and pressed a secret button. A lead donkey on the other end of the machine would whirl and kick the penny out of the dog's mouth into a slot, and the penny rattled away into the bottom of the bank. We emptied the bank again and again, using the same three pennies for hours.

Mrs. DeSalle had a wonderful house for children to visit. There were narrow back stairways that led around corners to the guest rooms and small building blocks made out of real brick smoothed down from years of children and grandchildren. My sister and I often spent the weekend indoors, building cities out of the bricks. There were only two bridges in the set, and we could never agree on where to put them. I favored a moat surrounding the city, like a castle. The inhabitants of my city fought to the death at its gates, holding the bridge against the oncoming hordes.

Sarah wanted a river to run through the heart of the city, with the bridges set like Japanese walkways. I teased her for being "mushy," but I was equally romantic with my bloody battle scenes.

Mrs. DeSalle had high tea every afternoon without fail. Not only were we children allowed to drink milky tea from her porcelain teacups, but her dog, Nat, was invited to join us as well. An old black lab with a cloud of white around his muzzle, Nat had his own plate with two cookies. Real cookies, not dog biscuits. He would eat delicately over his plate, never taking the cookies away to crunch happily on the rug as other dogs would have done. Mrs. DeSalle said that he didn't like dog biscuits and that he was old enough to eat exactly what he wanted, like herself. I had no idea how old Mrs. DeSalle was, but I knew she must be very old since she had a shock of white hair which stuck out around her head in tight curls, and my father always referred to her as "amazing." She mowed her own lawn and chopped her own wood for the fire. I'll never forget the story she told us of killing a giant tortoise on the front lawn by chopping off its head with an ax. She said that the body kept walking around for hours afterward, bleeding all over the lawn. I don't remember what a giant tortoise was doing on her lawn in the first place, or why she had to kill it, but it didn't seem incongruous at the time; that's the kind of woman she was. I only remember the image of the headless tortoise and Mrs. DeSalle easily wielding the ax above her white head.

On the self-kicking machine, human beings paid for the pleasure of being kicked like the penny into the mechanical bank. We asked the man behind the register when it had last been in working order, and he told us that it was broken when they got it, but they had bought it anyway.

"Kinda makes this place stand out," he said.

This seemed like quite an understatement, since the only competition was acre upon acre of evergreens. I bought some postcards, and we started up the mountain again. Within the hour we were at the top of Washington Pass. Artis's bus was pulled over into the rest area, and we pulled in behind him to see why he had stopped. It was the timing in the engine, and Artis was busy trying to work a miracle with a matchbook cover. I had seen that done with Volkswagen bugs but never with a school bus. Dmitri looked over his shoulder, and they talked buses while I searched for a significant sign that this was the top of the Continental Divide. There was no sign. The woods were too thick for any kind of view; it looked the same in every direction. The teenagers who were riding with Artis were squatting on the pavement, smoking cigarettes, so I went over to talk with them. I looked around the rest area. Here we were in the middle of the forest, and all of the humans were huddling together on a scrap of concrete.

Artis and Dmitri fussed over the engine long enough to declare The Nimbus ready to roll, and we all started out together in caravan. Artis had said that he wanted to stay with us in case he had any more engine trouble, and for a while we stuck together. The sound of heavy-metal music blasting out of his windows floated back to us down the highway. But after about an hour, he shot way ahead of us. No one could really bear to go at the pace of the grain truck except for Dmitri and me, though we did pick up speed going down the mountain, actually hitting sixty-five at one point.

Diablo Lake was a patch of sky reflected in the forest. The trees had been left intact around the lake, which was also a reservoir. Huge logging trucks spun past the lake carrying mammoth tree trunks, and I found myself falling asleep again to the rhythm of the trailer hitch thumping behind us. When I woke up, we were on the highway: Interstate 5. Four lanes of traffic streamed up toward the Canadian border. The plan was for all of the vehicles to rendezvous at a Denny's, one of the chain of highway restaurants that advertise "Open All Nite." All of the ve-hicles had to cross the border together because of the paperwork. There were other rules to the crossing as well: all of the minors had to be in the same vehicle as their parents. This meant anyone under eighteen, so the teen-agers had to vacate The Nimbus for more sedate vehicles for a little while. The grain truck was the last vehicle to arrive at Denny's, and everyone had just started to panic when we arrived.

Dmitri ran over to The Scenicruiser for a quick con-ference with Susan and Rebo. Since the truck was regis-tered in Dmitri's name, he would drive the truck and trailer through, hoping that no one would decide to search through all of the props and costumes for contraband. Susan would make the rounds before we left Denny's with a list of occupants of every vehicle, to make sure everyone was accounted for and that the children were with their parents. Once we arrived at the border, Rebo would go in and sweet-talk the customs officer with her honest Scandinavian face. What most of the group did not know was that if we were held up at the border and missed the last ferry out of Vancouver, we would definitely miss the next ferry to Quadra Island, and we wouldn't make it to our show. The chances of everything going quickly at the border were slim, and we just might end up with forty people sleeping on the side of the road. The Canadian side.

As we rolled up to the customs booth, the windows of The Scenicruiser were shut, so as not to draw attention to the disreputable crew inside. But it was hard not to draw attention to a forty-foot bus with an ugly rainbow stripe painted on the side and a back end covered with soot. Dmitri and I, in the grain truck, were separated from the rest early on. We had to go down a lane for trucks only, but we could see Rebo negotiating with the officer as we showed our passports through the other side of the booth. Dmitri is usually taken for a terrorist or a drug dealer at all border crossings, so Rebo pretended not to know him personally, even though our vehicle was listed along with all the others.

There were long lines of vehicles at the border that day. Maybe that's why we got lucky. Or maybe the officer just liked blondes from Minnesota. In any case, we were all waved on after only a short delay. Dmitri described the contents of the trailer with just enough detail to excite absolutely no interest in a customs officer, and they waved us on as well. In the rear-view mirror we watched The Scenicruiser start out at the same time, with a huge puff of black smoke, which must have made the officers think twice about allowing such a vehicle into their country. But it was too late. We honked happily at each other as we pulled out into traffic, and the whole caravan reunited on the road north to Vancouver.

Canada looked exactly like America except for the billboards, which advertised a different brand of cigarette. The joke going around was that we were not going to Canada but to "America Lite." Vancouver is a city built of glass skyscrapers wedged close to the sea and hemmed in by huge mountains, but we didn't stop to look. We were racing for the ferry out of town, across the Strait of Georgia to the big island, Vancouver Island.

We hadn't counted on another long line of cars waiting to get onto the ferry. Once again the last to arrive, Dmitri and I saw Max sitting shirtless on the roof of The Rubber Chicken. Artis was leaning out of the door of The Nimbus blowing soap bubbles, and Alex was passing sandwiches out of the window of The Scenicruiser. We seemed to take over everywhere we went, and it looked as if we might be here for a while. Dmitri and I wandered up to the buses and were just getting ready to have an espresso on Artis's stove when the line started to move, and there was a mad rush back to all of the vehicles.

The whole caravan made it onto the ferry, and we celebrated by taking over the main deck level. The day had gotten gray again, and it was colder out on the water. We all got cups of tea in the galley, and this time Alex appeared with a flask of brandy, which she passed around. We spiked our tea and leaned over the railing shouting at each other in relief. We were on the boat! The city we had never seen fell away behind us, and the air was wet and clean in our faces. I felt relieved at the drop in temperature and the arrival at the sea. I prefer a wide horizon to the darkness of the forest, which always unsettles me. The mountains of Vancouver Island loomed in the distance ahead of us. It must have been unimaginable to the first Europeans to climb the pass over the mountains into what is now the city of Vancouver and see so much water open up before them. It had to be another ocean. And then, when the clouds lifted, there were still more mountains ahead, floating above the sea like a mirage.

It was dark by the time we got to the other side of the strait. The caravan stopped for gas and headed north. There was one more ferry to catch from the eastern shore, about halfway up the island, which would bring us to Quadra and the gig. It seemed to me that it hardly mattered whether we made this next ferry or not. We had been hurrying so much all day that it had lost all meaning for me. It started to rain, and Dmitri kept the gas pedal to the floor of the grain truck, for what it was worth. Pretty soon we heard a distress call from The Rubber Chicken on the CB and found it pulled over to the side of the road just ahead of us. The headlights wouldn't work, and Max was underneath the bus on the wet pavement, searching for a loose wire. The Chicken was yet another old Karamazov tour bus that the Chautauqua had inherited, and Dmitri knew it pretty well. He checked under the dashboard and found that the switch to operate the lights had not been flipped on. Max, soaked all down his back with rainwater, started to laugh uncontrollably. Everyone was getting a little hysterical. We piled back into the vehicles and told each other shaggy-dog stories over the radio the rest of the way. I was secretly wondering how bad a motel room could really be if we missed the last ferry. I started to obsess quietly about cold, clean sheets and color television.

The ferry to Quadra waited for us. Rebo, once again, had charmed the powers that be, and though we rolled up a good twenty minutes late, they rearranged all of the cars to fit the grain truck and The Rubber Chicken aboard. It was a small boat going to a small island. The captain already knew about the Chautauqua, and he didn't want us to miss the ferry; his wife had bought tickets to the show the next day.

It was pitch-black and pouring rain at our campsite. An old fishing buddy of Dmitri's held a flashlight up to his face to say hello in the dark. The rain let up to a drizzle for just long enough to set up our tents. Dmitri grabbed our things out of The Scenicruiser and led me away. It seemed as if we walked a long way past the others, and I heard the sound of the ocean getting louder. Who cares about the view, I thought to myself, it's dark. Finally he stopped, dropping our packs and grabbing his tent.

"This is where I had my dream about you," he said. "Last spring. I came up to go fishing and camped right here. I had this dream."

"What was it? What was I doing?"

"I don't remember, but you were in it. I was in it. And we were here."

"In the tent?"

He laughed. "No. In the dream."

The next morning the wind woke us up, pulling hard at the corners of our tent. I unzipped the front flap, crawled out about thirty feet, and looked down. A few thin pines were growing out perpendicular to the cliff. There were dozens of bleached white logs on the beach below. A luminous gray mist lay on the water.

"Is there a way down?" I asked him.

"There's a path."

But by the time we made it to breakfast, we were already late to go to the show site. This was the day that I was going to have to raise the trapeze without Allen, and I worked on it all morning, taking a break only for the parade. Everyone was moving slowly after yesterday's marathon travel day, and nobody got to the show site on time. The day had started behind, and it stayed behind. The troupe was never able to catch up to the schedule we had made for ourselves. The parade, the workshops, and the show all ended up starting late, something that was not easily forgiven by the Quadra Islanders, as we later found out.

The ground was rocky, and it took some time to dig the holes where we were setting up the rigging. I swung the pickax over my head as the stage crew folded out the stage from the trailer and began to set up the lighting truss. The Rubber Chicken arrived and started to crank out coffee for the set-up crews. I realized that we had actually gotten pretty good at this routine, and I began to have faith that somehow the trapeze would get up, even without Allen, and it would be safe.

The parade was brief. A short march in a mini-shopping mall, the highlight of which was entering the grocery store and parading down the aisles while all the musicians shoved cans of food into their pockets, happily returning them at the cash register on the way out. Dmitri, Orbit, and I got right back to the trapeze and worked nonstop until it was finally in place. It took five hours, as opposed to one hour with Allen. There was a lot I had taken for granted, like Allen's knowledge of knots and his talent for finding places to tie off the rigging in the most desolate of show sites. In the end, we tied off part of the rigging to a tree as well as staking it down in the field. It took us all day, but when I finally got up on the bar, I felt safe.

A delegation of Chautauqua kids led by Ivan's seven-year-old son asked me for trapeze lessons, so I lowered the bar and spent what was left of the afternoon with them. They were utterly fearless, their rubbery bodies hyperextending in every direction. Even Sarah, who had been born unable to use her legs, let me lift her to the bar for a moment, and her upper body easily outdid the other children's for strength, if not agility. That was courage, I thought, as I placed her back on the ground. To hang from a bar above the ground with the certain knowledge that if you fell, you would fall to your knees, to your chest, to your face. I tried not to be overprotective and wanted more than anything to carry her to the ends of the earth if that's what she wanted. We became friends that day, and she stayed close beside me, her arms pulling her along on the ground as quickly as I could walk. She went through a lot of pairs of pants that way, her father told me, ripped them through the knees, but she got around as fast as the other kids.

We were told that the show had been moved up an

hour, to seven o'clock, and nobody was ready. There seemed to be constant miscommunications on Quadra, or maybe we were all just tired, but we had to scramble to make show time. The audience sat on folding chairs in the field facing the stage, while behind them the earth put on a glorious sunset. It was odd to have that many people gathered in a field, all looking away from the sunset, but it was better for us. The light in the sky was like footlights, casting everything in a wash of pink.

The event that came to be called "Garlic-Gate" didn't occur until the second act. Dmitri and Ivan did a musical juggling number using a marimba on wheels, which was elevated to the proper height for juggling so that they could easily reach the keys with a downward stroke of a baton, which they juggled simultaneously. We had all seen them do this act many times and were familiar with the build-up. They put on silly hats with bells attached to the corners, hung harmonicas around their necks, and—this was the clincher—each took a wad of dried-up old chewing gum from the end of the marimba and stuck it into his mouth. They chewed the gum madly as they played the marimba, juggled, played the harmonica, and tap-danced.

Tonight, moments after Dmitri put the gum into his mouth, he suddenly stopped his usual banter, and with a mixture of surprise and disgust he slowly removed the gum, looked at the band, and turned to the audience.

"I seem to have found a foreign object in my gum," he explained, as the band exploded in laughter just from watching his face.

"Ah . . . *garlic* gum." He looked meaningfully at Joe

Watts, the drummer, a likely suspect for any caper. "Ladies and gentlemen, excuse me." He turned his back and made terrible retching noises while facing upstage, then turned back to the audience with utter composure as he and Ivan finished the act.

Garlic-Gate was destined to become the defining event of this year's Chautauqua. Dmitri had no idea who had spiked his gum, and everyone had a theory. So many people were in and out of the backstage area before the show that it was possible for just about anybody to have substituted it for the preset gum unnoticed. Everyone, including myself, was held up as a suspect, but late that night talk turned to Toes Tiranoff—the tap-dancer. Toes was quiet and dreamy, with eyes that hid behind his wire-rimmed glasses and made him look a bit lost. He was the least likely person on the Chautauqua to pull a prank; therefore he was the perfect suspect. Toes was quite circumspect when questioned, but since he was always vague about everything, it was hard to know if this was really indicative of his guilt.

Every night Dmitri sat at his computer on The Scenicruiser to write up the schedule for the next day, which would be posted on a bulletin board and hung out the window of The Rubber Chicken. Everyone was supposed to take the time to read the schedule over breakfast. Most people never did, figuring they would follow the pack to the next event. On the night of Garlic-Gate, Dmitri, Rebo, Max, and I were all on the bus while Dmitri was making up the schedule. This is what we came up with for the next day:

4:30 AM—Breakfast in tents served by the children

5:00 AM—Aerobics

6:00 AM—CBS morning news "Good Morning Chautauqua"

7:00 AM—Free time—mandatory

7:05 AM—Meeting to discuss when to circle

7:10 AM—Circle to discuss meeting

7:23 AM—T yping W orqueshop—compulsory

8:15 AM—Tear-down and loading drill

8:45 AM—Band forms up

12 PM—Parade

1:30 PM—Roasted garlic luncheon served by Toes

1:52 PM—New scripts handed out for show

2:00 PM—New show rehearsal—lines memorized

3:00 PM—Garlic-Gate hearings—the Honorable Joe Watts presiding

4:00 PM—Toes Tiranoff sentencing and necktie party—formal attire required

6:00 PM—Presidential pardon for Toes Tiranoff —alas, too late

7:00 PM—Bingo game and Tiranoff funeral— local entertainment

8:00 PM—Sleight-of-hand lesson—today's lesson: "How to Resurrect a Tap-Dancer"

8:30 PM—Free time—optional

8:35 PM—Dinner—children served

9:00 PM—Sex and drugs without the kids

9:30 PM—Break camp and drive 5,000 miles to catch ferry to a train where we cross a one-lane bridge over a huge chasm without lights and with no clothes for eight AM set-up for a show which no one will attend. Thank you!

10:00 PM—Circle to discuss the schedule

By the time Dmitri and I reached The Rubber Chicken for breakfast the next morning, everyone had read our schedule and was discussing the trial. Artis the Spoonman was to be the prosecutor. He paced around in his patchwork vest with a maniacal grin.

"Where were you on the morning of Garlic-Gate?" he would demand as another sleepy soul arrived for breakfast. He threw back his head and laughed at their confusion as he slammed down another espresso. Joe Watts was to be the judge, because of his cold-blooded nature, and Magical Mystical Michael wanted to be the defense attorney. Toes Tiranoff basked in the attention. Bewildered at his sudden ascent to stardom, he wandered about with a silly grin and giggled when pressed as to his innocence. Magical Mystical Michael walked him back and forth around the campsite, arm around his shoulder, advising him to say nothing. Officially, Chautauqua had the day off, but everyone was pumped up for the trial. There had been an actual Circle scheduled for the morning, however, as the only required event of the day. I assumed it was to be some sort of spiritual gathering. It was set for eleven o'clock. We figured there would still be plenty of time for the trial after we had (quickly) become One with Everything.

The Circle turned into a meeting that lasted four hours. Most of that time was spent discussing whether or not we were having a "meeting" or a "Circle." A Circle was supposed to be free of business and logistical discussions; a time for bonding or working through emotional issues. A meeting was to talk about the nuts and bolts of Chautauqua, the organizational end of things. On that day, it was neither. It was simply an endless discussion about what we should be discussing, and we never broke out of our own self-consciousness. Every time one person started the group in one direction (discussing matters either spiritual or practical), somebody else would throw up a roadblock, and we would be back to discussing what it was proper to discuss. After four hours of this, not even the most ornery members of the group could keep it up, and the meeting/Circle dissolved with people finally wandering off in disgust. Most of the "day off" was gone, and everyone was in a bad mood.

The trial never happened. We had spent too much time staring at each other in a circle to be able to envision spending any more time in a group situation. Dmitri and I escaped to the beach. I squeezed a fresh lemon stolen from the kitchen into my hair and lay on a rock in the sun. Dmitri knew enough to leave me alone for the moment, so he made us sandwiches from chunks of local smoked salmon and juggled with Max, who had brought some clubs down to the beach. Rebo sat on an unapproachable rock. It seemed as if everyone who came down to the beach that afternoon wanted to be alone and take refuge in the physical. If we had only had the trial and simply play-acted together, we would have achieved the "bonding" that the Circle tried to engender, without the forced aspect of it that had poisoned the gathering.

That night Dmitri borrowed a car and took me out to dinner. It was a big restaurant at the fishing resort, with bottles of wine wrapped in white linen and waiters who walked quietly between the tables. I felt like a clod. I had tried to dress up, but everything was slightly wrinkled and smelly by this time. I must have gone to the bathroom eight times just to run hot water from the tap over my hands and face. We didn't talk about Chautauqua. We talked about our families and past loves and killed a bottle of wine between us. We took hours over our meal, both of us feeling like Cinderella at the ball. We left the restaurant as they were starting to blow out candles at the other tables, and left a big tip. Down by the cliff, the rain stung our faces as we bent into the wind. Our tent was still dry, and we fell asleep almost immediately, wrapped in our envelope of blue nylon.

In the morning the Quadra natives met us with boats for a fishing and boating expedition. It was to be our last day on the island. Dmitri and I went on a boat geared up for salmon fishing, as he was a fisherman and already familiar with the waters around Quadra. A professional fishing guide loaded us into his skiff with as much foul-weather gear as we had been able to pull together. There were long docks with "Live Bait" signs hung over the end to attract boaters poking through the mist as we went by.

I missed Angela just then and wished that she had come with us, but she didn't see the point of getting up that early just to go fishing. There were no commercial fishing boats in sight, and our guide told us that almost everyone out in a small boat was a serious sport fisherman who had flown to the island just to go salmon fishing from the resort with a guide like himself. This kind of fishing was an expensive hobby, and we were being treated like royalty to get this kind of expedition for the asking.

Dmitri lit a Cuban cigar, though it was only eight-thirty in the morning, and cast out his line. I didn't expect much from my own line, having never fished before, but there is always that kernel of hope. When my line jerked once, then again, I just about went out of my skin. Then the line tugged hard, and Dmitri and the guide declared that yes, there was indeed a fish on my line. Now *they* nearly jumped out of their skins, yelling advice to me every thirty seconds to let it run, pull in a bit, let it run again. I was thrilled. Could I actually catch a fish? I suddenly understood why people fished. This was as exciting as anything I had ever done before, and I was surprised at how much I cared now that there was a fish on the line. It made perfect sense to me that people would fly across the country and spend hundreds of dollars for a moment like this. I kept wanting to see the fish, but it wouldn't come to the surface.

"It's a big one," they assured me. "Give him a lot of line, even when he's tired, then reel him in."

"How do I know when he's tired?"

"He's not tired yet." People who know what they're doing always give you cryptic answers like that.

So I let out some line. The fish kept pulling. Now the entire boat was focused on my fish. Suddenly the tension in my line lessened by half. I looked over at Dmitri.

"He must have let go," he said. "Reel it in."

"No," I said as I started to reel. "He's still on there." My rod was bending over again.

"Maybe he's tired," Dmitri said, getting ready with the net over the side of the boat. "Just keep reeling him in slow."

"That's a good-sized fish," said the guide, eyeing my rod. Then suddenly it was coming up, not in the flash of silver that I had expected, but in a flash of orange. As it got closer to the surface, I pulled it in next to the boat— an enormous six-armed starfish was jammed onto my hook, its eye a dark bead in the center of its body.

Dmitri and the guide both started talking at once. They had never seen anything like it. My first fish. The guide took the hook out of the starfish with professional gentleness and threw it back. I watched it spiral down into the dark green water, cold and passive.

"That starfish put up quite a fight." The guide said it with what could have been admiration.

Dmitri went on to catch a nice-sized salmon that day, and I caught a second starfish.

"Two starfish in one day—never happened before," the guide kept saying as we pulled in our lines and sped for the beach, where all of the boats carrying Chautauquans were converging for a community picnic. I didn't know you could catch starfish with fishhooks. As children, Sarah and I used to peel them off the rocks and pilings in New

England. I had the image of a big salmon grabbing my hook and running with it for a while, then unhooking himself when he got bored and popping a nearby starfish onto my line as a joke.

Most of the Chautauquans had been sailing a big catamaran that was already anchored off the beach, and Dmitri added his salmon to an ice chest filled with the big silver fish. There were more slabs of salmon roasting over a fire, and a man with a big black beard asked for volunteers to gather oysters. I didn't know you could just pick oysters up off the beach; I thought they came in round trays filled with chipped ice at parties a couple of times a year. But there was an oyster bed down the beach, he said, so Angela and I grabbed a cardboard box to fill up and headed off. Nothing I had ever seen on the beaches of New England prepared me for the oyster bed. It went on for half a mile of shoreline along a little spit, piles of gnarled white shells with curled lips that came together like a toothless cartoon grin. We didn't even have to look for them; all we did was reach down and gather them up. We hauled the cardboard box back when it was bursting at the seams, and the oysters were thrown onto the grate just as they were, to cook in their own juices.

Dmitri wouldn't eat oysters because they weren't kosher. I hadn't known that he was kosher until that moment. The cuisine was so simple on Chautauqua that I hadn't even noticed him avoiding pork and shellfish.

"It's easy for me," he said, almost apologetically. "I'm already a vegetarian, or, rather, a fishetarian."

I had never known anyone who actually kept kosher

before, and I didn't really know the laws. I had been to "dairy restaurants" on the Lower East Side of Manhattan, but I didn't really know what that meant either, other than good, cheap food. Anything with fins and scales was OK, Dmitri told me now, but you can't cook meat in the same pot as dairy products. All of this stuff goes back to a time when the Jews were trying to define themselves as a tribe apart from others and Judaism as different from the polytheistic religions surrounding it in the Mideast.

"It was a way for the leaders to say: 'See those guys over there? They eat pig, so we don't,' " he explained. "It could have been as much about maintaining an identity as about health issues. Though everybody knows you can get bad diseases from pork if it's not cooked right. I can't be absolutely strict, since I'm on the road all the time. But I try to keep kosher."

"But why? These laws are totally arbitrary, you said so yourself." I was sucking down another oyster, which was hot and steamed to perfection. It didn't need any lemon, and cocktail sauce would have been an obscenity.

"It's just a discipline." He laughed. "I guess it just makes me feel like a good Jew."

"Yeah, well, you know what would really make you a good Jew?" asked Magical Mystical Michael, who was standing nearby eating a second plateful of everything.

"What?"

"To join my brother and me in a game of beach croquet."

Magical Mystical Michael's brother was visiting for a few days. His teenage daughter had been along on the whole Chautauqua, under the not-so-vigilant eye of her Uncle Michael. Her father was dark where Michael was blond, and though he had also grown up in the Bronx, he now lived in Boulder, Colorado, and spoke without a trace of an accent. Magical Mystical Michael had been out of the Bronx for twenty years, but he still sounded as if he were from down at the corner.

One of the Quadra natives had brought croquet mallets and a couple of tennis balls. Beach croquet consists mainly of whacking the ball as hard as you can back and forth along the beach. There are no wickets, but someone had built a series of sand bridges that the ball was supposed to scoot through around the course. Whenever the ball went under a bridge, however, it got stuck halfway, and the bridge was destroyed. When all of the bridges had become piles of sand, Magical Mystical Michael declared the game to be at an end.

"We won!" he yelled, throwing his mallet into the air.

"What?"

"Sure. First one to destroy the game wins, right?"

. . .

"Salmon again?" the kids had started to ask. Alex laughed as she prepared salmon patties for tomorrow's lunch. It was only later that we found out that the people of Quadra Island, despite their hospitality, felt ill-used by the Chautauqua. The parade had been late by almost an hour, and the workshops did not begin at the time listed in the paper. These transgressions were taken very seriously by the Quadra Islanders, who were far from being laid-back country folk. The Chautauqua was not invited back the following year.

But that night the Quadra Islanders seemed content as the band played Turkish music until the moon came up over the finger of beach where we were feasting. Theories about Garlic-Gate went late into the night, but Toes was as enigmatic as ever. His newfound stardom was beginning to take on a kind of cult status. Toes Tiranoff was coming into his own.

We were off and running first thing in the morning. The Quadra Island ferry left only twice a day, and we had to make the morning boat so that we could catch a second ferry, which ran from Canada down to the San Juan Islands at the northern edge of Puget Sound. We were headed for Orcas Island, the largest of the small chain of islands that mark the water boundary between Canada and the United States. Orcas Island was our last stop before Port Townsend, where the tour would come to an end. There were only five days left, but it felt longer because we had to do five shows and travel hundreds of miles before it would be over.

We caught the ferry off Quadra and arrived early, for the first time, to catch the next ferry to Orcas. While we were waiting in line for the ferry, Benjamin and Anton, both from the saxophone section, got an accordion and a metal cup out of the bus. Anton put on a pair of sunglasses, and immediately they were transformed into Adolfo and Giovanni, the blind accordion player and his monkey. They walked up and down the line of cars, Benjamin skittering along on his haunches and rattling the cup.

As soon as they heard Adolfo's Italian accent, Dmitri and Angela had to get into the act. Dmitri became Paolo again, of Paolo and Francesca's Ristorante Italiano, while Angela defended the honor of Milo's across the street. Angela complained in Italian that Adolfo and Giovanni were bad for business, and Paolo signed up as their manager and demanded payment from Milo's for the entertainment. A loud mock-Italian argument ensued, interrupted by bursts of accordion music from Adolfo and screeches from Giovanni.

We could have gone on like this for hours, but when a man in a sky-blue uniform walked over to us, we figured it was time to keep it down. Surprisingly, he didn't tell us to be quiet but asked for our identification. Dmitri and Benjamin were caught without their wallets. They had left them on the vehicle they had been traveling in as far as the ferry. They started to go back to Artis's bus to get them when the officer stopped them: "I'll ask you some trick questions."

Dmitri and Benjamin stopped; now they were nervous.

"Where were you born?"

They answered, mystified.

"Thank you very much." He turned and walked on past us, toward the bus. We saw his shoulder patch as he turned: U.S. Immigration. We had thought that we went through U.S. customs on the other side, but then we saw the officer heading to The Scenicruiser.

"Has anyone here bought anything while in Canada?" he asked at the front of the bus.

Joe Watts looked up. "I bought this book, but it isn't very good."

That was it. We were through customs. The whole troupe. It had been hardly noticeable, and after the big build-up to get over the border to Canada, most people thought we still had to get through some other examination on Orcas Island. But it never happened.

Once we got all of the vehicles onto the ferry, the band took out their instruments and started to play on the deck. Other passengers watched, finally venturing out onto the deck to dance. Pretty soon the whole boat was dancing, the older couples outdoing the younger ones in their ability to high-step and twirl. Toes Tiranoff, still under heavy suspicion, tap-danced along with the band, the hollow metal deck making a great sounding board for his taps. An older woman came up behind him and followed every step. Her face was achingly alive while Toes's had that strangely vacant, inward state he fell into when he danced. The ferry ride lasted for an hour and a half. Toes danced the whole way, and the band kept playing all the way back to the United States.

CHAPTER
9

ORCAS ISLAND FELT like a return to civilization. Friends met us there to see the show, now that we were close enough to Seattle to be visited. Orcas may be quiet in the winter, but it was packed in the summer. There were bicyclists everywhere, riding thick-tired bicycles weighted down with huge saddlebags carrying camping gear. It didn't look like much of a vacation to me as they huffed down the road in packs of ten, sweating in their neon spandex.

The Chautauqua was being presented by a local arts organization, and they had planned to have us camp at the show site, a large field in front of an elementary school. There was a community center as well, with a small stage and an old piano. As soon as we arrived, the kids went tearing through the place. Suddenly all of them were running back at us, screaming, and we saw the yellow jackets buzzing around them. They had run into a nest in an old couch on the back porch. Some stingers were still sticking into their skin. We all ran for the children, brushing off the insects and pulling the children into our arms and onto the bus. Sasha, a seven-year-old with short blond hair cut like a pageboy around her little face, got it the worst. She cried and cried as someone applied lotion to her swellings. All the children were crying, and for a while it was impossible to tell who had actually been stung.

The entire campsite was infested. Yellow jackets are actually carnivorous. They sting you in order to kill you and eat you, Ivan informed us with macabre cheer. There were nests all over the ground, and we had no choice but to set up our tents carefully among them and try to mark the nests with fluorescent tape. There was nowhere else to camp at the height of the tourist season. Sasha walked around with red welts on her arms and face for a few days, and everyone in the troupe got stung once or twice.

The weather turned cold and windy that night, so nobody gathered under the torches at Fyodor's tent, a centrally located four-man mansion. After dinner everybody scattered. The kids were taken to the movies to cheer them up, and everyone else was either tent-hopping or already in bed. I ended up sitting on the tailgate of Psycho Car with Angela, sharing a bottle of brandy. She was talking as if the Chautauqua were already over, and we both began to get maudlin when Dr. Dennis, who had flown in to join us for the closing of the journey, came by and got us laughing again. Angela, however, was firmly committed to having a good cry that night, so she took her brandy bottle off to find Rebo, who, she knew, was at least as sentimental as she was.

Dr. Dennis and I wandered over to The Scenicruiser, where Dmitri was sitting up late in front of the computer. Dennis wanted to know all about the "Is this a Circle or a meeting?" discussion on Quadra Island. Dmitri was worried that all the fun was going out of Chautauqua. In Dennis's opinion the whole Chautauqua should spend the next summer doing a mindless physical activity, like digging an enormous hole and then filling it in again. The group had to stop and relearn how to simply communicate and coexist, he said, and the task that we performed together was really of no consequence so long as it was physically exhausting.

Dmitri couldn't imagine doing Chautauqua without the vaudeville show, and besides, he said, who would pay the bills? It was the show that pulled people in, and then they got exposed to the workshops, and slowly the Chautauqua was getting its message across. "But what exactly is the message?" asked Dennis. Dmitri wasn't sure; maybe there shouldn't be just one message but a lot of different messages, and a way of life. "Find the money somehow," said Dennis, "and dig a ditch."

I let them talk, playing with a wooden puzzle Dennis had brought for Dmitri. It was a rectangular box with a hole in one end and an unseen maze inside. There was a marble trapped inside. I had been flipping it over and over in my hand for two hours. The marble rolled out into the palm of my hand. There was a moment of stunned silence.

"You know what?" I said. "Dennis's idea isn't as crazy as Dmitri thinks it is, and Chautauqua isn't as screwed up as Dennis thinks it is."

Neither of them could think of anything to say to that, so we went to bed.

In the morning I walked around the show site with Dmitri, Abe, and Max, trying to decide where to set up the stage trailer. We had to consider where the sun would be at show time so that it wouldn't shine directly into our eyes while we were performing onstage. Abe also had to approve the site in terms of electricity to run the lights; he wanted to avoid using the generator because of the noise of the engine. After they talked it over for forty-five minutes, it was decided to leave the trailer exactly where it was—close to the school and the electrical outlets. It didn't look as if the sun was going to come out; the sky was dark blue with spurts of rain that came and went all day.

The rest of the morning was spent setting up the trapeze. "Ground not too hard," reads my diary. Allen had rejoined us, as promised, and the trapeze was up before the noon parade. There was a strong wind coming in from the southeast, so I decided to do my warm-up as quickly as possible, before the parade. Wind frightened me more than anything else. I knew that I had been lucky so far. Excepting the first night at Rosalie's place, I hadn't been forced to cope with any high winds. The wisest thing to do was not go up there if the wind was really blowing, but I hated to cancel a performance. I had that inbred actor's doggedness about performing. I couldn't miss a show unless

I was dead or in the hospital. I was prepared to push it to the edge of safety tonight.

By the time we got downtown for the parade, the little harbor was bright with white-capped waves, and all of the streamers that hung from the storefronts were blowing straight out into the street. The town was a little too cute. The houses were New England—style and had fresh coats of paint. It looked like a town that made all of its money in the summer months. There were ice-cream parlors and espresso bars in every other doorway, and lots of blond teenagers anxious to serve customers.

The parade was a huge hit, at least partly because the main street was filled with tourists glutted with ice cream and waiting for something to happen. The bus attracted a lot of attention, as usual, just by pulling up at the end of town, and when the band started to form up and march down the street, the tourists went wild. It seemed as if everyone we went by on the sidewalks joined in behind us and followed us to a village green, where the band kept playing salsa music with brief interruptions by Dmitri making announcements about the show.

Despite the parade, there was a poor turnout for the show that night. The weather continued to be ugly, and the people who did come wore their rain gear and brought tarpaulins to sit on. The storm never broke over us, but the clouds were low above the fir trees that ringed the show site. I spent the first half of the show inside the elementary school (the only place that was heated), stretching and staying warmed up for my act. I could watch the show through a big picture window, and everyone onstage looked like a brightly colored stick figure. There was a man sitting and reading in the classroom when I came in, but he never said a word. I felt self-conscious, stretching out in my dirty red tights, which I wore over my costume to keep warm. He never once looked up.

I was nervous about performing in front of my friends from Seattle. It's always much worse to perform for people you know, and I generally ask people not to tell me which night they are coming when I am doing a show. In this case, they were camping overnight with us, so it was impossible not to be aware of them as I shivered behind the stage trailer at intermission. The rain was still holding off, but my bar swayed slightly in the rising wind. Then Magical Mystical Michael went on to do my introduction, and I stripped off my tights, ready to go. Once I began, I didn't feel the cold anymore, but the bar was swinging more than usual. It was impossible for me to tell whether it was wind or nerves, and I couldn't spend any time thinking about it. My performance passed by in a blur, and I was glad to be back on the ground when it was over.

"Your bar was swinging a lot," Dmitri whispered as he stepped back for me to leap from his shoulders and take my bow. "I was scared."

"Me, too," I whispered back, still smiling at the audience.

I took my bows and ran behind the stage trailer to strap Magical Mystical Michael and Dmitri into the double strait-jacket. The rest of the show went well, and the audience loved the juggling at the end, as they always did. I felt depressed, so when Allen and I took down the trapeze right after the performance, it was a good excuse for me not to socialize after the show. I had not risen to the occasion as I had wanted to despite the wind, and I felt embarrassed to see my friends. They wouldn't know the difference, of course, never having seen my act before. But my own sense of the performance dictated my mood, as it probably always will. Allen, Orbit, Dmitri, and I were still taking the gear apart by the time everyone else had gone to Fyodor's tent under the tiki torches. I went to pick up a late dinner that Alex had hidden away for me. I could never eat before a performance, so I had started saving food for afterward. Cold stuffed green peppers and rice looked as if they had been good when they were hot.

Up by the tiki torches, Dmitri was passing a flask of whiskey around. There were members of the Royale Famille DuCaniveaux visiting, and they were the best company you could ask for around a campfire. The whiskey warmed us up, and we made enough noise to have to be shushed by the neighboring tents at about one in the morning.

Alex wandered over and told Dmitri and me that while she was packing up the kitchen for an early departure, she had noticed that the trapeze poles were not strapped to the roof, as they usually were. Hadn't Orbit and Allen said they would take care of that? Didn't they always? Well, they hadn't, and it had to be done tonight, for the bus was leaving at dawn to get in line for the morning ferry. There was no one else to do it, so Dmitri and I left Fyodor's pavilion to strap on the poles in the dark. We hardly spoke as we hoisted them up onto the roof and lashed them down.

"We're going home tomorrow," Dmitri said as we crawled into our tent. Home? Wasn't this tent home? Wasn't The Scenicruiser home?

"Are you scared?" I asked, reaching for him.

"Yes," he said, and kissed me. We kissed until we couldn't hold onto consciousness any longer, lips slipping off each other's mouths.

It took two ferries to go from Orcas Island to Port Townsend. The first one, a large commuter ferry, brought us to the town of Anacortes on the mainland. It looked very industrial from the highway, with a big oil refinery spewing white smoke. From Anacortes you could catch the interstate north to Vancouver or south to Seattle. We turned west on the small road to the Keystone ferry, which went on a short run between Whidbey Island and Port Townsend on the northeastern tip of the Olympic Peninsula. To get to Keystone we had to drive over Deception Pass, twin canyons with water rushing every which way at the bottom. It is a tricky pass for sailors. There is not only the main current, which sweeps through the middle of the channel, but currents that actually run counter to the tide, making the water swirl and chop up unexpectedly. The pass is narrow, rocky, and beautiful. The road went across the top of it on a high bridge like a railroad trestle. I was riding in The Scenicruiser, and the bus felt as if it were teetering over a swing bridge in the Andes. The water looked far away; a motorboat was slowly beating ahead against the current.

"These currents can turn you right around or stop you dead in the water," Max said. He had been raised around here and had navigated the pass in a sailboat. "I've seen boats try to get through for hours with the engines cranked up full, going against the tide, until they ran out of gas and had to drift or sail back home."

Once over Deception Pass, we were on Whidbey Island itself, home to an air force base with the accompanying billboard: "Pardon our noise, it's the sound of Freedom." We had heard the jets ever since we got close to the island, and once we were on the ferry out of Keystone, which wasn't even a town, just a ferry landing, I saw a squadron flying low to the water in a V-formation. The high scream of the jet cut through the heavy sound of the ferry engine.

The ferry was an older, smaller model than the boat from Orcas to Anacortes. It had wood paneling inside and real brass railings that were cool to the touch and had worn to a dull shine. On the walls were old black-and-white reproductions of early ferry runs and logging towns. They were all logging towns in those days, inhabited by bearded men in hats who stood solemnly over enormous trees for the camera. The towns had mud for streets and long rafts of logs bound together in the harbor. There were never any women in the pictures, but I knew they were there; behind the camera, behind the doors, or behind the bar at the local tavern.

I went to the rail as Port Townsend came into sight. The red brick buildings got prettier as we got closer, and a big gray building on the bluff over the town looked like an old town hall, but Dmitri told me it was the post office. Port Townsend is a small town that was built on a grand scale in the late nineteenth century. Speculators had thought that it was where the West Coast railway line was going to end. It was already the port of entry for all of the ships from the Far East and Alaska, and the town's founding fathers envisioned a modern metropolis surrounding the harbor, with trains headed down the coast to California laden with the essences of the East and the Northwest: silks and salmon.

As it turned out, the railroad went to Seattle and from there north to Vancouver, where it joined up with the Canadian Pacific Railroad bringing grain from Saskatchewan. Port Townsend became a ghost town with a main street of four-story Victorian buildings with huge bay windows looking out on the water. As Seattle grew, Port Townsend remained forgotten until the 1970s, when it became a sort of haven for hippies and artists who wanted to leave the city or couldn't afford to live in it. They changed the character of the town somewhat, but it still felt like Steinbeck's Monterey back then. The artists were struggling to get by, and they lived together at the Town Tavern; almost all of the artists who still live in Port Townsend seem to have started out there. In the seventies you could arrive in town and be pretty confident of getting a job at the Town Tavern. In lieu of cash, there were crash pads upstairs and the opportunity to eat all you wanted at the deli downstairs.

The Town Tavern was the only place I had ever been in Port Townsend. I had gone along for the ride in the late seventies with some friends whose band was playing there. I was still underage and looked even younger, so they wouldn't let me in the door of the tavern despite my pleading that I was "with the band."

My girlfriends took me upstairs to the crash pad and teased my hair. I piled on makeup, put on sunglasses, and switched outfits. We smoked a joint, and I was ready to try again. This time the bouncer let me in, though I'm sure it was more because they admired my chutzpah than because anyone was really fooled.

Now the Town Tavern is a regular bar with a good pool table, and most of the artists have their own homes. There are still a lot of artisans and hippies in town, but it has the feeling of a tourist stop rather than a forgotten mill town. "Victorian Bed and Breakfast" signs are all over town, and the tourist industry keeps the little shops along Main Street going. The paper mill just outside of town is still the only viable industry, but it doesn't cost that much to live in Port Townsend, which boasts of being the wooden-boat-building capital of America.

"Is the Town Tavern still there?" I asked Dmitri, who had come up behind me as the town loomed closer and closer.

"Yes. But I've never been there."

The ferry took its last turn in toward the dock, and we ran to get into our vehicles. I sat at the front of The Scenicruiser, and Dmitri drove. I had once been to Arcadia, the Karamazovs' seventy-five-acre spread outside of Port Townsend, but this was different. Now I was going to the place that Dmitri had called "home" last night. When he left Arcadia at the beginning of the summer, it had been home to Anita as well, until she got Dmitri's phone call from Montana. He didn't know where she had gone now. When she moved up here, had she left no bridges back to her other life? I couldn't understand this. In New York City, people often don't give up the leases to their apartments even after they're married. Why had she moved in with him so quickly?

"We needed to be together," Dmitri had said briefly. "And I'm never anywhere."

The Scenicruiser drove up the long driveway toward the big red house with the name "Arcadia" lettered across the front. It is an old house, built in 1908. A red barn stands behind it with the Karamazovs' heart and wings, the insignia of the group, painted on the front. This is their rehearsal space, which was in the process of being con- verted into a public performance hall. Dmitri pulled the bus into the large lot next to the barn and got out quickly, avoiding the hordes of questions that were being thrown at him. He grabbed my hand and walked toward the house. Neither of us knew what to expect. A strange blond woman was loading her car beside the kitchen door. She gave Dmitri a dirty look and kept packing.

"She's been running the inn since Anita left," he ex- plained, walking by her without speaking. He lived on the top floor of the house. I stopped him at the stairs.

"Don't you want to go up alone?"

"No," he said, and I could see that he was scared. When we got to the door of his bedroom, it was locked, and he had to try every key on his ring before he found the one to unlock it. We couldn't see through the glass door because of a dark blue sheet thrown over it. I sat awkwardly on the bed in the foyer outside his bedroom, and he apologized, explaining, "I've never locked this door."

The main thing I remember is the flies, the way they hung in the center of the room, spinning around one another. You would have thought there would be a breeze that high up, on the third floor of the inn, with the mountains all around. Something strong, like a slap across the face of the house. But there wasn't any air at all, though all of the windows had been left open. So the flies just kept spinning themselves to death in the exact middle of the room, halfway between the floor and the ceiling. Probably one or two of them had already dropped to the floor, but then they were lost, for the floor was covered with rose petals.

It seemed that after dragging the mattress onto the floor, she must have smashed everything down on top of it. All available surfaces, the bookcases, and the big table would have been easy to clear in one sweeping motion of rage. The desks had imploded onto themselves, and piles of paper teetered at the edges. Broken bits of candles and edges of pottery slashed through the dried flowers. They were mostly rose petals, dried rosebuds and loose petals of different colors with—this surprised me— no scent.

This was the room where Dmitri kept his books and his found things: rocks he had picked up, he no longer remembered where. He traveled a lot. I didn't want to know the woman he had left in this room. I didn't want to look at the half-torn photograph that had been dropped on the wreckage. Her face was pretty, smiling, against the green hills of another country.

We stood there not talking, and I started to cry. I could taste her pain in my mouth as the tears ran down my throat. He found a cardboard box and dragged it to the center of the room. There was really nothing to say. We started to gather the bits of glass and flowers and colored cloth. Occasionally he stopped as he recognized an object. I hardly stopped at all. Only when I found something intact and asked him if he wanted it. Porcupine quills stuck into the rug and pierced the flower petals. I pricked myself and thought of Sleeping Beauty as I watched the globe of blood swell on the tip of my finger. That night we took the cardboard box to the woods and burned it. He prayed in Hebrew for forgiveness and redemption.

The next day Pop Wagner got a horse for the last parade, a tall Appaloosa done up in Western gear. I insisted on climbing up behind Pop to stand on the rump of the horse in my bare feet. The trapeze artist should always ride the horse in the circus parade, after all. I had a picture in my head, and Pop was game for anything. I held onto Pop's shirt with one hand and waved with the other. It felt as if everything were coming true until the horse decided to move two steps sideways, and I was on the ground. I fell straight to the asphalt, landing on my right hip. I was up immediately, with nothing broken, but I had to settle for sitting on the back of the horse and waving, while Pop twirled his lariat. By the end of the parade I could feel my thigh and hip joint stiffening ominously. We had matinee and evening shows scheduled for today and tomorrow.

The main street of Port Townsend was lined with Victorian buildings covered with old advertisements faded like frescoes on the outside walls: "Owl Cigars 5 cents;" "Pepsi Cola." It looked a little like a movie set with the enthusiastic townspeople standing in the doorways and waving. It all seemed too good to be true. The Karamazovs were hometown boys in Port Townsend, and the Chautauqua usually sold out the 1,500-seat tent outside of town where the show was put on every year. It would be our biggest audience of the tour, and I loved the thought of doing a trapeze act under canvas—even green canvas.

Early that morning we had raised the trapeze rig inside the tent, which was quite a trick. The tent was set up on cement, so it was impossible to dig the holes necessary for the feet of the rig. Allen drove the truck axles right through the cement for stakes and set up blocks at the feet of the poles. There were rows of chairs already set up inside, and we had to lash one of the trapeze poles to a huge steel pipe, which supported the tent itself. When the wind pulled at the sides of the tent flaps, the pole shifted slightly, and that made me nervous. We guyed out the rig as much as possible to compensate, but the top of my poles almost grazed the roof of the tent. In desperation we eventually tied off a line to the roof of The Rubber Chicken.

The tent was at an old army base whose grounds had been turned into a state park once it had been determined that the Japanese and the Germans were not really going to invade us, and the bunkers facing the Strait of Juan de Fuca were covered with moss and ferns. Some of the buildings had been given over to the arts, and we had the luxury of a backstage that was indoors with a large mirror and plenty of chairs. All of the old barracks were wooden with windows covered by green shutters that flapped back and forth. There had once been forty enlisted men sleeping in the room where forty Chautauquans now primped and warmed up and gossiped.

The fort sat on a green hill overlooking a hook of beach that cupped the edge of the town. At the end of the beach was a lighthouse surrounded by a chain-link fence. There was a house, and I wondered if there was still a lighthouse keeper there; perhaps the fence was for his dogs. A line of fir trees, which looked like palm trees from far away, grew along the farthest edge of the hook. Their lower branches had been blown off into the ocean long ago, and they leaned their long bodies out naked below a topknot of green. Surrounded by the old-fashioned barracks, we could have been on any U.S. base in the 1940s; Guantánamo Bay or the Philippines.

I had started to apply a homeopathic ointment for bruising to my leg as soon as the parade was over, and all through the day I kept peeling down my tights to apply more of the gel to my discolored skin. The bruise was spreading like a small lake over my hip, and it hurt to sit on the bar. Between shows I never stopped moving, terrified that it would freeze up completely, and I wouldn't be able to perform.

The matinee was a little rough, but matinees usually are, especially in a new space. We played to a sold-out crowd for both shows, and the audiences loved it. It was a warm night, and the evening show was one of the best of the tour. The tent enclosed it in a way that concentrated energy without reducing it. The canvas was just enough of a boundary between our event and the outside world. We didn't have to tear down that night, since we were coming back tomorrow, so we were free to go to Arcadia and start a bonfire. Rebo Flordigan sang some sad songs around the fire, and I cried listening to her. I felt transparent. Dmitri took me into his own bed for the first time that night. I hadn't been able to sleep in his room the night before, and we had set up our tent outside with everyone else. Tonight I tried to think of it as his bed, not their bed, and I didn't want it to be my bed.

The last day of shows was hot and bright, and I had the privilege of a long, private shower in Dmitri's top-floor suite. I tiptoed around the bathroom like a thief. Nothing I could think of was going to stop him from breaking me the way Anita had broken his room apart. I took my shower alone, letting the water wash over my body for a long time. I walked the fields around Arcadia all morning and then slept until show time that afternoon. It took the band marching through the tent flap up onto the stage to wake me up fully for the matinee. My last thought before falling asleep had been whether I would be able to walk the next morning, but my leg was only slightly stiffened, and though I still had a slight limp, I knew I could perform.

The second-to-last chance, I said to myself as I pulled on my white tights, which were gritty from yesterday's performances. Everyone seemed to be feeling it. There had been more talk of Garlic-Gate around the fire last night, and a rumor was flying that all would be revealed at the final Circle tomorrow.

People I had hardly spoken to for the whole tour came up and said hello, asked how I was, and I found myself doing the same thing. Pop gave me a rope lariat of my own, and I got a lesson in twirling it like a cowboy. Between shows Alex made us a vegetarian gourmet dish with stuffed mushrooms as an entrée. Someone had bought a bottle of wine and was passing it out in paper cups. I couldn't eat before a performance and didn't dare to drink. The matinee had gone well, but I was favoring my bruised leg and hadn't been able to feel completely confident. Rosalita, my partner in The Daring Devianté Sisters, was coming from Seattle to see the show tonight, and I wanted my performance to be good.

People were ready for the last show before they needed to be. Jan was our timekeeper, and she walked around at a quarter to the hour with nothing to do. People were already in their band jackets and stupid pants, ready to go. The show started at eight o'clock exactly, which had never happened before. Ivan blew the short blasts on his bandleader's whistle that set the tempo, and the band kicked into the last entrance of the summer.

Inside the tent everything was darkened to a dim green light. The walls shut out the sun, which wouldn't really set until after ten o'clock, and when the tent flap was lifted to admit the marching band, a triangle of sunlight filled with dust fell inside and lit the band in silhouette. Once onstage, the players went wild. The drum section swayed back and forth, knocking into one another and pulling faces. Two of the drummers wore red noses, and they had a mock battle with the horn section during the opening number; no one was holding back. The band never stopped razzing the individual performers, and the dialogue between the orchestra pit and the acts took up more time than the acts themselves. When Eric, a gardener who led a workshop in the afternoons, came onstage to change the scenery, he was hit in the face by a pie. Magical Mystical Michael opened the lid of his levitation box, and a flock of balloons escaped to the roof of the tent. The audience knew they were seeing us make each other laugh, and they loved it.

I chalked my hands over and over before going up that night. There was hardly any room backstage, and I had to crouch down behind the stage until the moment when I climbed onto Dmitri's shoulders for my entrance. He first gave me a kiss, then his hands and back for a ladder. This time I didn't even feel my bruise during the performance, and out of the corner of my eye I saw my shadow on the tent wall, silhouetted by the spotlight: the trapeze artist. I am the trapeze artist. I could think about it for only a split second, and even that was dangerous. It was time to swing, pause, switch hands, and kick up. I blew kisses to the audience, found Rosalita and blew one just for her. She knew exactly how much work it had been for me to be up there. What she didn't know was that I had been doing this performance just for her.

The Karamazovs outdid themselves that night. Dmitri got more garlic planted in his gum, but it was almost to be expected at this point. Smerdyakov, the member of their troupe who didn't go on Chautauqua, came up from Seattle and took part in the show, and they had a grand juggling finale with torches and popping champagne bottles. Once more we got a standing ovation. The band played song after song after the show was over, not wanting to let go, and we all danced, pulling the audience up onstage and leaping into the aisles. Around the bonfire at Arcadia we sat up late telling "true stories," or stories that anyone could pass off as true. That night Dmitri burned sage in his room, to purify it, and we made love for the first time since we had arrived at Arcadia.

Breakfast was late and subdued as we gathered for the final Circle in the barn. The barn was being slowly renovated by the Karamazovs. It had an old dance floor and big windows facing out over the fields, where the mist still hung like a shroud over the alfalfa. Susan started by filling in the other eye of the wooden doll she had presented at our first Circle and passing the doll around. It had ended up with a quizzical expression, as if it were not quite sure where it had landed. The sage and the eagle feather were brought out of Dmitri's pouch and passed around again. The kids coughed into the sage smoke, and the East Coast people made jokes about it, as they always did. I realized that I had come to take burning sage for granted, and that in itself made me feel miles from home. I looked around the Circle and thought how little I really knew of these people and how intimate they were with me. There were some I would never have met if it had not been for the Chautauqua, as well as some I would rather not have spent the last month living with on the road. There were some I hadn't been able to get to know, and it all felt as if it were happening too soon to be over already.

I was flying home in a few days, and Dmitri was leaving tomorrow for the Karamazovs' regular tour of the East Coast. It no longer felt strange to me to be sitting beside him in the tribal circle, but once we left, anything could happen. We would see each other next in some coffee shop in New York, or in the darkness of my kitchen on the Lower East Side, which faced the bottom of a shaftway.

We went around the Circle, and everyone had a chance to speak. Many said it was the hardest Chautauqua they had ever been on—that they hadn't felt the bonding they were looking for. I thought that if they hadn't been trying so hard to bond, it might have just happened. Like the trial for Garlic-Gate. Magical Mystical Michael surprised most of us by giving a detailed deposition explaining the mystery. Toes Tiranoff was exonerated as Magical Mystical Michael revealed that it had been Eric, the gardener, and he who had planted the gum on Quadra Island, though Alex, the cook, was possibly guilty by association, since she knew who had taken the missing garlic and was therefore party to the crime. The pie in Eric's face at the final show had been revenge for the deed, though only a few people were in the know, and Dmitri had been convinced of Toes's guilt until now. Hours passed as we went around the Circle, and several people cried. There were lonely people who had never felt a part of anything before, and angry people who felt they deserved more from Chautauqua.

When my turn came, I was circumspect, unable to draw it all into a nutshell for these intimate strangers. What could I say about watching events quiver and burst like mercury inside my heart? I had been strung out taut and high with another—The Other—as we drove, packed, slept, didn't sleep. Eyes and mouths and hands inside each other too much for sleep. I looked down at my calloused palms, said, "Thank you for having me," and didn't cry.

That night Dmitri packed, and he was gone at five the next morning to catch his plane. By midday Arcadia was almost deserted. Rebo, Max, and Susan were there, but Angela had to be back at work in Seattle and had left before I woke up. The night before we had exchanged addresses and promised to write, like children at the end of sleep-over camp. I was one of the few people staying one more night. I took a bucket and a sponge and went out to clean The Scenicruiser. Packs of cards lay split open on the bunks, and the smell of sour milk rose from the rug in front of the refrigerator. I opened the windows and began at the back of the bus with the blue room, working my way toward the driver's seat. I collected all of the lost things: a child's bathing suit, a set of parade music, a pair of stupid pants that was stuffed behind a bunk, and some poker chips. I held my breath and opened the refrigerator door, holding the sponge at arm's length as I dug into the hideous spilled substances that lined the inside. But it was good to clean the bus, and I felt like a hero as I ventured into corners and cupboards that even the Chautauqua had never used. Leaving something as concrete as a clean surface behind helped me to feel that Chautauqua was really over, and as I brought my plunder to the growing pile of "lost and found" in the barn I felt protective about everything finding its way home again.

I lay awake that night in Dmitri's bed, which was surrounded on three sides by curtainless windows. Dmitri called home after his performance, and it felt strange to be answering his phone. I could already hear the city in his voice. The wind pulled the clouds in great black hunks past his windows all night, and it seemed as if the moon hardly moved at all. The temperature had dropped, and the tree frogs sang the same song over and over again. There was foxfire in the fields as the sky went from black to gray that morning. It had become fall, suddenly, and I needed to feel pavement under my feet again. I left for the airport before anybody was awake. As I always expect things to end without warning, I have never learned how to say goodbye.

EPILOGUE

ONE YEAR LATER, Dmitri and I were married at Arcadia. That same year I fell from my trapeze while performing a double act with my partner, Rosalita, at the Country Fair. My left arm was badly broken, shattering the elbow and breaking the wrist. Because of the permanent damage to my arm I have not been able to perform on the trapeze since the accident. At least, not yet . . .